ISBN 978-0-243-38920-9
PIBN 10796542

# 1 MONTH OF
# FREE
# READING

## at
## www.ForgottenBooks.com

---

By purchasing this book you are eligible for one month membership to ForgottenBooks.com, giving you unlimited access to our entire collection of over 1,000,000 titles via our web site and mobile apps.

To claim your free month visit:
www.forgottenbooks.com/free796542

English
Français
Deutsche
Italiano
Español
Português

# www.forgottenbooks.com

**Mythology** Photography **Fiction**
Fishing Christianity **Art** Cooking
Essays Buddhism Freemasonry
Medicine **Biology** Music **Ancient
Egypt** Evolution Carpentry Physics
Dance Geology **Mathematics** Fitness
Shakespeare **Folklore** Yoga Marketing
**Confidence** Immortality Biographies
Poetry **Psychology** Witchcraft
Electronics Chemistry History **Law**
Accounting **Philosophy** Anthropology
Alchemy Drama Quantum Mechanics
Atheism Sexual Health **Ancient History**
**Entrepreneurship** Languages Sport
Paleontology Needlework Islam
**Metaphysics** Investment Archaeology
Parenting Statistics Criminology
**Motivational**

# THE DEIFICATION OF LINCOLN

By

## IRA D. CARDIFF

*Author of*
*"A Million Years of Human Progress"*

The Christopher Publishing House,
Boston, U. S. A.

PRINTED IN THE UNITED STATES OF AMERICA

# DEDICATION

*To those lovers of truth who are unafraid of special interests, public opinion or popular superstitions, this little volume is respectfully dedicated.*

# ACKNOWLEDGEMENTS

Grateful acknowledgement is due the following publishers for use of certain quotations in the work:

CENTURY CO., New York, "Lincoln's Parentage and Childhood" by Louis A. Warren.

DAUGHTERS OF THE AMERICAN REVOLUTION, DECATUR CHAPTER, Decatur, Ill., "Personal Recollections" by Mrs. Jane Martin Johns.

DODD, MEAD & COMPANY, New York, "Lincoln the Man" by Edgar Lee Masters.

HARCOURT, BRACE AND COMPANY, New York, "Abraham Lincoln: The Prairie Years" and "Abraham Lincoln: The War Years" by Carl Sandburg.

KNOPF, ALFRED A., New York, "Lincoln on the Eve of '61" by Henry Villard.

M. E. CHURCH SOUTH (Abingdon-Cokesbury Press), New and Nashville, "Confederate Echoes" by A. T. Goodberk

PUTNAM'S SONS, G. P., New York, "Abraham Lincoln—Man of God" by Hill.

SCRIBNER, CHAS., SON, New York, "Interpretation of Poetry and Religion" by George Santyana.

TRUTH SEEKER, New York, "Six Historic Americans" by John E. Remsburg.

WAKEFIELD, SHERMAN DAY, New York.

*Men in all ways are better than they seem.  They like flattery for the moment, but they know the truth for their own.  It is a foolish cowardice which keeps us from trusting them, and speaking to them the rude truth.*

*Emerson*

# INTRODUCTION

Biography is a form of history. It is the history of an individual and his relation to his environment. To evaluate this relation, and from it draw any valid conclusions, the truth should be known and delineated by the biographer. This calls for a mind scientific to the last degree, a mind devoid of prejudice and preconceived notions of its subject, a mind which has respect for the truth and the courage to portray it, a sense of relative values, a mind sufficiently analytical to discriminate between the essential and the trivial regardless of how interesting or sensational the latter may be. It is, of course, not maintained that all matters of trivial character should be omitted, for they often may be used to stimulate interest, also may throw considerable light upon character. Care is necessary, however, lest they detract rather than add to the thesis.

Albert Britt in "The Great Biographers" states of biography, "The beginnings were crude . . . . . Saints and martyrs, of course, were usually the objects of biographical effort and the writer was committed in advance to a process of deification that has not yet disappeared."

Britt might have added that this process reached its zenith in the last half of the nineteenth century, for English speaking peoples. Also around the pinnacle of this hyperbolic zenith revolved the satellites who perpetrated their fancies and fantasies upon a gullible and defenseless public in the form of Lincoln biographies, so called. This habit of deification mentioned by Britt is an outgrowth of the propaganda which has ever been such a disagreeable feature of the Jewish-Christian Religion and which has contributed greatly to its downfall.

In extenuation, however, it must be pointed out that the biographer is confronted with many difficulties and temptations. Not only is information of his subject often difficult to obtain, but his sources are apt to be contaminated with prejudice, patriotism or propaganda. Also the whole truth is, oft times, unobtainable and the biographer is tempted to supply the missing portion from his imagination. Then, too, he is strongly tempted to produce a work which will please his publisher and yield him financial return. "The curse of art is, it has to be financed." As the reading public becomes more discriminating, it is hoped that some of these handicaps may disappear.

Concerning Lincoln, all of these and many other crimes have been committed in his name, and the popular mind has formed a complex of such a nature that no ordinary evidence or exposition can hope to correct.

# The Deification of Lincoln

ILL-FATED LINCOLN! How troubled and annoyed he would be if he could today listen to the animated controversies over his parentage, his religious beliefs, his prayers, his youthful love affairs, his marital troubles, his poverty (or prosperity) in his youth, etc., ad libitum, ad infinitum, *ad nauseam.* Still his annoyance might change to edification, if not entertainment, as he learned of the sterling qualities, mental and moral, of Thomas Lincoln, his supposed father, whom it now appears was quite industrious and prosperous; learned of the chastity of his mother and grandmother; of his own piety and his great interest in "evidences" of Christianity, also discovered that he "spent most of his time upon his knees in prayer while in the White House." Would he be pleased, or otherwise, to learn of his deification, to discover that whatever he accomplished was a result of the guiding hand of a god and not from his own ability or moral worth?

It might also strike him as somewhat singular, if not remarkable, that people who never knew him, never saw him, some even having been born since his death, should know more about such matters than did his private secretary, his chief of staff, his law partner and most intimate friend, or his wife; in fact more than he himself did. Some *readers* may also be struck with this remarkable anomaly—SOME; not many! In fact most readers—and especially *listeners*—are not at all interested in the truth about Lincoln. They are not interested,

11

in other words, in the real Lincoln. They desire a supernatural Lincoln, a Lincoln with none of the faults or frailties of the common man, a Lincoln who is a savior, leading us to democracy and liberty —though most of said readers (and listeners) are not interested in democracy or liberty—except for oratorical purposes. That this is true is too patent to need any proof; or if proof is demanded, we only need point to the several thousand romancing biographers and biographies. If the public did not buy the latter, they would not be produced. In fact, a biography of Lincoln which told the truth about him would probably have great difficulty in finding a publisher. In other words, the romancing biographer is the one who is read.

It is one of the strange and puzzling features of human psychology that the truth is so often unpleasant and unacceptable, or perhaps more correctly that the truth is unpleasant to so many people, only a small minority being interested in it. Is it the hangover of Neolithic blood still coursing in our veins? Or is it still older, a Simian tendency to play, to imitate, to make believe? Perhaps, in the case of Lincoln, these atavistic tendencies are also accentuated by the mass psychology which has been generated by the politico-religious oratory of the Lincoln Day programs. Most "information" of Lincoln is thus obtained. The orator of such occasions is rarely a student of Lincoln. He is invariably a lawyer or clergyman. If the former, he is primarily interested in advertising himself; if the latter, he is interested in proving Lincoln a devout Christian—and otherwise dispensing propaganda for his own particular brand of religion. In either case, the result is the apotheosis. (Such orators acquire most of their information from listening to themselves talk.) This condition has continued for a couple of generations until the speaker or writer who does not deliver an apotheosis when discussing Lincoln is set down as dull and uninteresting, if not uninformed or unpatriotic. Thus Lincoln has come to be our most abused, most misunderstood public character.

Biographies in general are more often the reflection of the passions and prejudices of the biographers than a revelation of the truth concerning the subject. There is nothing the average individual cherishes so much as his prejudices. The ordinary man will fight much longer and harder for them than he will for the truth. With reference to Lincoln, prejudices have been intense, hysterically acquired and tenaciously adhered to. Pre-conceived notions have predominated in the minds of biographers and readers alike. These, supplemented by the greed of conscienceless publishers and advertisers, have created a deplorable mess concerning our beloved Civil War president.

*     *     *

Abraham Lincoln was in many respects typical of a rather picturesque portion of early American society, especially the pioneer period of the Ohio Valley. He eventually found his place as a practicing country lawyer of rather ordinary ability and moderate success. He possessed little or no cultural background and an education meagre even for that date. On the other hand, his integrity was far above that ordinarily found in the profession. His mind was analytical and logical, and his personality picturesque and attractive. Possessed of a good memory and some ability for impersonation, he became an adept politician and a rather clever vote getter. His humble origin, his human interest and his rational mentality, stimulated by his readings of Voltaire, Paine and Jefferson, made him a champion of human freedom, an anti-slavery partisan and incredulous and critical of orthodoxy.

Lincoln's first real education was derived from his law partner, William Herndon, a man of exceptional ability, with an exceedingly active interest in subjects scientific and philosophical. The scientific age was in its infancy, growing, expanding and revolutionizing the thought of the day. Herndon kept in touch with this, and discussed it with his ever interested senior partner. Then there entered the intellectual life of Herndon the cultured and scholarly Theodore Parker, with his humanitarian and unorthodox ideas, which also secondarily had their effect on Lincoln.

Following this preliminary education, Lincoln was confronted with the opportunity of debating the issues of the day with the erudite and clever statesman, Senator Stephen A. Douglas. The education which Lincoln received in this campaign gave him some equipment for meeting the political problems which followed.

As an administrative head of a great nation in a time of stress, he was not an unqualified success. "The President (Lincoln) is an excellent man, and in the main wise; but he lacks *will* and *purpose,* and, I greatly fear he has not *the power to command."* (By Ed. Bates, from his diary 12/31/61, relating how he urged Lincoln to be commander-in-chief in fact as well as in name. Bates was Attorney General in Lincoln's cabinet.)

"The President knows as well as I do, that General Butler's proceedings to overthrow the civil law at Norfolk, and establish his own despotism in its stead, is unlawful and wrong, and without even a pretense of military necessity, and yet, he will not revoke the usurping orders, for fear

General Butler will raise a hubbub about it. Alas! that I should live to see such abject fear—such small stolid indifference to duty—such open contempt of constitution and law—and such profound ignorance of policy and prudence!

"My heart is sick, when I see the President shrink from the correction of gross and heinous wrong because he is afraid 'General Butler will raise a hubbub about it.'" (Bates diary Aug. 4, 1864—pp. 393-4.)

Lincoln's homely ways, his human sympathy, his integrity and sincerity greatly endeared him to many of the people and his tragic death at the acme of his success consummated his popularity. While his passing will ever remain one of the tragedies of the nation, it was only the beginning of the tragedy which was to follow his memory for—there is no telling how long.

The unthinking public (the great majority is unthinking) has ever failed to realize that because a man holds an important office or occupies a highly important position, he is not necessarily a great man. People have a habit of elevating to such positions men who are very mediocre in mental make-up. (In a democracy they are doubtless representative.) The people then expect great things of these men and if, through a combination of circumstances, unusual progress in statecraft or successful war during the tenure of one of them, is made, he receives the credit for these as *his* achievements; he becomes a popular hero, even though he may have had no more to do with the matter than the bit of driftwood which rides the waves has in causing the wave. If the position be a public office, the man's friends and political hangers on, by clever propaganda, cultivate this attitude on the part of the public.

If, further, the office holder in question, happens
to have had a lowly origin—came from the no-
bodies of society—there is a deal of satisfaction to
the unthinking host. The affair is looked upon as
a vindication of democracy and a salutary re-
buke to the highbrows who may have at some
time been guilty of original thinking—for, after
all, no one is more unpopular than a thinking man.

\*    \*    \*

Lincoln receives credit for the successful prose-
cution of a great war, for the preservation of the
union, for the abolition of human slavery and for
telling a good story. To the latter he is entitled to
the credit accorded. To the three former—well, let
us see. Did the South ever have a chance of winning the war? Never! Pitted against it was a North
of immense material resources and wealth, a much
greater population than the South, a population
more energetic, more resourceful and better educated, thus a larger and better equipped army,
officered by several quite superior generals; therefore the ultimate outcome was inevitable.

The preservation of the Union was a natural consequence.

As to the abolition of human slavery; within the
century previous, human enlightenment had devel-
oped to a point in Europe and America that such a
gross violation of man's natural rights as human
slavery had become repugnant to the mass of mankind. At that time, the intense struggles of the
American and French Revolutions were fresh in
the minds of the people and the thought of a
human being treated as a piece of property to be
trafficked as a mule or a hog was offensive to all
sense of decency—even to most Southerners. In
fact, the slave owners of the South were relatively

few in number, though powerful politically on account of their wealth and social prestige. The passing, sooner or later, of the atrocious institution of
slavery was, therefore, also inevitable.

That Lincoln played an important and service-
able part in these epoch making events goes without saying. That in so doing, he displayed at times
great skill and tact, also great human sympathy
and tolerance is to his credit, but to say he was the
causative agent in the abolition of slavery or the
preservation of the union is absurd.

This fact may be further illustrated by an epi-
sode related by General Stewart. On New Year's
Day, 1861, General Charles Stewart, of New York,
was calling upon Senator and Mrs. Douglas, in
their fashionable *Minnesota Block* home in Washington, D. C. The General says,

"I was making a New Year's call on Senator
Douglas; after some conversation, I asked him,

" 'What will be the result, Senator, of the efforts
of Jefferson Davis, and his associates, to divide the
Union?' We were," said Stewart, "sitting on the
sofa together when I asked the question. Douglas
rose, walked rapidly up and down the room for a
moment, and then, pausing, he exclaimed, with deep
feeling and excitement:

" 'The Cotton States are making an effort to draw
in the Border States, to their schemes of secession,
and I am but too fearful they will succeed. If they
do, there will be the most fearful Civil War the
world has ever seen, lasting for years.'

"Pausing a moment, he looked like one inspired,
while he proceeded: 'Virginia, over yonder, across
the Potomac,' pointing toward Arlington, 'will become a charnel-house—but in the end the Union
will triumph. They will try,' he continued, 'to get
possession of this capital, to give them *prestige*

**abroad,** but in that effort they will never succeed; the North will rise *en masse* to defend it. But Washington will become a city of hospitals, the churches will be used for the sick and wounded. This house,' he continued, 'the *Minnesota Block,* will be devoted to that purpose before the end of the war.'

"Every word he said was literally fulfilled—all the churches nearly were used for the wounded, and the Minnesota Block, and the very room in which this declaration was made, became the 'Douglas Hospital.'

" 'What justification for all this?' said Stewart.

" 'There is no justification,' replied Douglas.

" 'I will go as far as the Constitution will permit to maintain their just rights. But,' said he, rising to his feet and raising his arm, 'If the Southern States attempt to secede, I am in favor of their having just so many slaves, and just so much slave territory as they can hold at the point of the bayonet, and no more.' "

Senator Douglas was a wise, far-seeing, patriotic statesman. He died during the early years of the war and never received his just deserts historically on account of having opposed Lincoln in their celebrated debates, for after Lincoln's death and the people became hysterical over him, they could see nothing good in Douglas. He, with other discerning statesmen, foresaw the inevitable outcome of a conflict between the North and South.

In fact if any single individual is to be given the credit for saving the Union, the honor should probably go to Miss Anna Carroll, whose skillful and untiring efforts, between the time of Lincoln's election and his inauguration, prevented the District of Columbia and Maryland from falling into the hands of the secessionists. Later she furnished the plans (at a most critical time) which resulted in the

Union victories at Donaldson, Shiloh and Island Number Ten. Her influence with Lincoln was such that she was frequently referred to as the unofficial cabinet member.

*     *     *

The United States is a young nation. Its first and greatest crisis was the Civil War. Lincoln occupied the center of the stage during this crisis. While his record as an executive may not have been a brilliant one, he, nevertheless, made few glaring mistakes and his motives were, for the most part, above reproach. After his tragic and untimely death, which occurred at a time when the people were hysterical and unreasonable over national matters, it was but natural for the unthinking populace to more or less deify him. However, the *popular* opinion or estimation of a person in high position is usually meaningless. Mark Twain puts the matter thus, "To my mind, the bulk of any nation's opinion about its president, or its king, or its emperor, or its politics, or its religion, is without value and not worth weighing or considering or examining. There is nothing mental in it; it is all feeling, and procured at second hand and without any assistance from the proprietor's reasoning powers."

Few prominent characters of history have been more atrociously misrepresented than Lincoln. Few have been more vilified than he. Few have had a fair name and honorable career made more ridiculous with exaggerated praise than the Civil War president. It has fallen to his unfortunate lot to be the victim of a greater variety of picturesque hysteria than any other historical character. In the long record of humanity's foolish mental capers, there exists only one other comparable to it, namely the psychological contortions in regard to Christ, but since Christ was scarcely an historical character, this leaves Lincoln still victim number one for being the most misrepresented.

The hysteria in regard to Lincoln has been so pronounced, so persistent and so wide spread that anyone attempting to make a sincere and comprehensive appraisement of Lincoln must take cognizance of it, and, if possible, explain it. What, therefore, is the genesis of all this hysteria? It may be grouped under four main heads—

Lincoln's lowly origin;
his ancestry;
his heterodox views on religion;
the method of celebrating his birthday anniversary.*

A brief consideration of these may be worth while. Taking them in order, it is interesting to note that up to the time Lincoln was nominated for president, little or none of this hysteria existed. He was a man among men—respected for his tolerance and fairness, for ability somewhat above the ordinary, for his lucid and logical thinking, for a considerable amount of courage and firmness, for his human sympathy and for his liberal views anent the natural rights of man. That he was well regarded by his neighbors is evidenced by their having elected him to the Illinois legislature several times, to Congress once, and came within an exceedingly narrow margin of electing him to the United States Senate. He also received the overwhelming endorsement of his state for the presidency. His associates of the bench and bar held him in high esteem both for his integrity and his fairness. He was not thought of by his neighbors as a phenom-

---

* Recently the use of Lincoln's name by a large commercial company, in the vulgar racket of advertising, has furnished a further list of myths and fables to add to the hysteria.

enally unusual man in any respect, and he did not think himself an exceptional man.

Also in his neighborhood he was well regarded, even by his political enemies. In fact, a perusal of all that has been written of the man previous to his nomination to the presidency fails to reveal any pronounced antagonism—any attempt to vilify him; nor was there, on the other hand, any disposition to apotheosize him at that time, and his nomination for president was not the result of a widespread and popular demand as many of the "biographers" would have us believe. What, then, produced the sudden change?

For a decade previous to Lincoln's nomination for the presidency, there had been more or less acrimonious discussion of the question of negro slavery, a question which might have been amicably settled had it not been for the few extremists on each side. Lincoln was not one of these. His attitude was one of moderation and compromise; so much so in fact that his attitude on human liberty was, at times, somewhat inconsistent and illogical, as he would strongly advocate complete and unqualified natural rights for men (even advocating suffrage for women, a radical and revolutionary doctrine for that day), yet would admit that he did not favor the ballot and full rights for the negroes. In fact, in a speech at New Haven as late as March, 1860, he advocated allowing slavery to remain where it then existed.

With Whitney's invention of the cotton gin near the close of the eighteenth century, the production of cotton became profitable. Its culture called for much menial and arduous labor under a subtropical sun; thus the ownership of slaves became economically very profitable. Previously slavery had not been especially advantageous or popular either in

the north or south. However, with the enthrone-
ment of Cotton as King, there arose an oligarchy of
large slave holders who operated great plantations
at handsome profits. This few thousand large and
wealthy slave-holders was the government of the
South—in fact, pretty much of the nation at times.
The opposition to this domination of the national
government by these Southern Aristocrats was one
of the contributing factors in the prolongation of
the war. Certain Northern politicians were determined to rid the government of this Southern domination, and abolition of slavery with the concomi-
tant economic wrecking of the South would accomplish it.

These Southern ruling aristocrats were, many of
them, descendants of the Cavaliers who settled Virginia. They were Royalists by nature and had little
patience with the frugal and industrious Puritans
and Roundheads of New England or the hard working German and Irish imigrants of the north. They
were for the most part wonderfully fine people, but
with a viewpoint and a background so totally different from that of the Northerner that a reconcilia-
tion of the two was virtually impossible.

Accustomed to lording it over the negro slaves,
they soon came to assume a more or less similar attitude toward the less fortunate whites of the
South, who became, in the eyes of the large slave
holders, the "poh white trash." These Southern
aristocrats looked with contempt upon anyone who
worked with his hands—did any work a "niggah"
could do.

This peculiar psychology of selfishness and arro-
gance was greatly strengthened and encouraged by
the organized church, which repeatedly demon-
strated, by means of the "divinely inspired word,"
that slavery was O.K. and the slave owners were

treated as the salt of the earth.* This Southern aristocracy thus formed a social set-up conducive to much intolerance and fanaticism, making the slavery question one exceedingly difficult with which to cope. Concomitantly with this profitable exploitation of human slaves, there arose a certain amount of atrocious abuse of these unfortunate negroes, which aroused in some non slave owners a strong feeling of resentment and protest with certain retaliatory methods of affording relief to the negroes, e. g. the underground railroad. There also arose the very important national question of the *extension* of slavery with a certain amount of legislation on the matter—the "Missouri Compromise," "The Kansas and Nebraska Bill," "The Dred Scott" decision, et alia.

On each side, the extremists fanned the flames of conflict between the two elements—the extremists of the North being known as abolitionists. In the South the abolitionist was regarded as the most contemptuous being in existence.

Lincoln was not an abolitionist, though as soon as he was elected president he was denounced as such by the southern extremists. Also the railsplitter's reputation, so valuable to him in the North, branded him, in the South, as "poh white trash." He thus immediately became an object of contempt to the Southerner, or at least the ruling Southerner. It was freely stated the South could never tolerate a "poh white" in the White House. It demanded a "gentleman." The press and pulpit of the South let loose torrents of calumny and abuse of the man before

---

* To many of the present day, this may seem strange; however, it was not, for the church upheld slavery (of whites) in Scotland until the time of the French Revolution (1807). "In 1783 the managers of the Society for the Propagation of the Gospel absolutely declined, after a full discussion, to give Christian instruction to their slaves in the Barbadoes." Lecky, Hist. Eng. in 18th Cent.

he had time to take office, and, like all such emotional outbursts, the vilification became unreasonable and exaggerated to a ridiculous degree.*

---

* An editorial by E. Pollard of the Richmond Examiner, published at the time of Lincoln's inauguration, reflects a southern view, and this is rather mild and conservative as compared to others, as follows:—

"The Presidential ticket nominated by the Black Republican convention in 1860 was Abraham Lincoln, of Illinois, for President, and Hannibal Hamlin, of Maine, for Vice President. Governed by the narrow considerations of party expediency, the Convention had adopted as their candidate for President a man of scanty political record — a Western lawyer, with acuteness, slang, and a large stock of jokes, and who had peculiar claims to vulgar and demagogical popularity, in the circumstances that he was once a captain of volunteers in one of the Indian wars, and at some anterior period of his life had been employed, as report differently said, in splitting rails or in rowing a flatboat.

"The circumstances attending Lincoln's journey to Washington to be inaugurated and his advent there were not calculated to inspire confidence in his courage or wisdom, or in the results of his administration. . . . . In the speeches with which he entertained the crowds that, at different points of the railroad, watched his progress to the capital, he amused the whole country, even in the midst of great public anxiety, with his ignorance, his vulgarity, his flippant conceit, and his Western phraseology. The North discovered that the new President, instead of having nursed a masterly wisdom in the retirement of his home at Springfield, Illinois, and approaching the capital with dignity, had nothing better to offer to an amazed country than the ignorant conceits of a low Western politician and the flimsy jests of a harlequin. His railroad speeches were characterized by a Southern paper as illustrating 'the delightful combination of a Western country lawyer with a Yankee barkeeper.' In his harangues to the crowds which intercepted him in his journey, at a time when the country was in revolutionary chaos, when commerce and trade were prostrated, and when starving women and idle men were among the very audiences that listened to him, he declared to them in his peculiar phraseology that 'nobody was hurt,' that there was 'nothing going wrong,' and that 'all would come right.' Nor was the rhetoric of the new President his only entertainment of the crowds that assembled to honor the progress of his journey to

With this Southern attitude toward Lincoln's humble origin, many in the North also sympathized. This attitude formed a tremendous handicap to the new president, a handicap which he never was able to overcome. It effectively prevented any possible mediation of the differences between the North and South.

Leaving this aspect of the Lincoln hysteria for the present, let us turn to the second cause of the same, i. e. his ancestry. Lincoln, at one time, confided to his most intimate friend (and lawpartner for quarter of a century), that his mother

---

Washington. He amused them by the spectacle of kissing, on a public platform, a lady admirer who had suggested to him the cultivation of his whiskers; he measured heights with every tall man he encountered in one of his public receptions, and declared that he was not to be 'over-topped'; and he made public exhibitions of his wife—'the little woman,' as he called her—whose chubby figure, motherly face, and fondness for finery and colors attracted much attention.

"These jests and indecencies of the demagogue who was to take control of what remained of the government of the United States belong to history. Whatever their disgrace, it was surpassed, however, by another display of character on the part of the coming statesman. While at Harrisburg, Pennsylvania, and intending to proceed from there to Baltimore, Mr. Lincoln was alarmed by a report, which was either silly or jocose, that a band of assassins were awaiting him in the latter city. Frightened beyond all considerations of dignity or decency, the new President of the United States left Harrisburg at night, on a different route than that through Baltimore; and in a motley disguise, composed of a Scotch cap and military cloak, stole to the capital of his government. The distinguished fugitive had left his wife and family to pursue the route on which it was threatened that the cars were to be thrown down a precipice by secessionists; or, if that expedient failed, the work of assassination was to be accomplished in the streets of Baltimore. The city of Washington was taken by surprise by the irregular flight of the President to its shelter and protection. The representatives of his own party there received him with evident signs of disgust at the cowardice which had hurried his arrival at Washington."

was an illegitimate child of a prominent Virginia planter. This may not have been true; however, there is little doubt that Lincoln thought it true. There is also considerable evidence to the effect that Lincoln himself was the natural child of Nancy Hanks and a prominent, capable and respected citizen of western North Carolina, Abraham Enloe. Whether either Lincoln or his mother or both were illegitimates mattered little so far as the post election furor was concerned. Nothing could fit into the campaign of calumny against the man so well as the ugly word "bastard." In a time and a society saturated with religious hypocrisy and political prejudice, no better setting could have been devised for the distortion of the truth or the perpetuation of a falsehood. Nor was it to be expected that political and religious fanatics would be fair enough to acknowledge that Lincoln had no choice in the selection of his ancestors, or further, that he was probably a much superior man as a result of this unconventional parentage, for there is little evidence that any good ever came from Thomas Lincoln, his apparent father. Lincoln once said he didn't know who his grandfather was but was more interested in knowing what his grandson would be. Would that the public could have been as sensible.

However, it mattered little where the truth lay in regard to Lincoln's ancestry. His traducers welcomed any irregularity which could be used to besmirch his life; therefore the story was used to the utmost.

Turning now to the third cause for Lincoln hysteria, we must consider his heterodox religious views. That Lincoln was throughout his life highly unorthodox is beyond question. He was not a member of any church and rarely attended any re-

ligious services. That he was an avowed and outspoken infidel in his younger days seems also true.
In fact, he wrote an essay in which he came to
much the same conclusions as Voltaire and Paine,
of whose writings he was a frequent reader. When
Lincoln ran for Congress, his opponent was Rev.
Peter Cartwright, the celebrated evangelist, and
Cartwright used Lincoln's infidelity against him
during the campaign with persistent emphasis,
though at election time, the people of the district,
by an unprecedented majority, expressed a prefer-
ence for the infidel over the divine. Again when
he was a candidate for president, twenty out of
twenty-three of the ministers of his home district
were opposed to him on account of his unorthodox
views, which views are apparent from the following statements by Lincoln:

"When you show me a church based upon the
Golden Rule as its only creed, then I will unite
with it."

"What is to be, will be, and no prayers of ours
can arrest the decree."

"The dogmas of the past are inadequate to the
stormy present."

"The Churches, as such, must take care of themselves."

"Still, in addition to this, there is something so
ludicrous in promises of good or threats of evil
a great way off as to render the whole subject with
which they are connected easily turned into ridi-
cule."

"Friends, I agree with you in Providence; but
I believe in the Providence of the most men, the
largest purse, and the longest cannon."

"It will not do to investigate the subject of religion too closely, as it is apt to lead to infidelity."

"I never tire of reading Paine."

"There was the strangest combination of church influence against me. It was concluded that no Christian ought to vote for me, because I belonged to no church."

In fact, up to the time of Lincoln's candidacy for president, there is no record of his ever having made any statement which would in any manner indicate the slightest religious belief. His earlier speeches contain no reference to a god. While such an attitude of mind is what one would expect from a man who championed human freedom, nevertheless the intolerance of Christianity is such that it could not condone such beliefs. There was, therefore, furnished another indictment against the man. He was an *infidel*. To the pious, fanatical and selfish Southern slave holder, Lincoln thus epitomized about all that was undesirable—"POH WHITE", ABOLITIONIST, BASTARD, INFIDEL! To the Southerner, and many of the Northerners as well, this represented an impossible set up. The hysterical condition of the country at the time (1860) prevented any fair or rational view of any of these matters and Lincoln labored the remainder of his life under this tremendous handicap.

\*    \*    \*

With Lincoln's death came a marked change of sentiment. Perhaps one should more correctly say a change of hysteria. For a year or more previous to this it became apparent that the cause of the South was lost—that Lincoln and his policies were succeeding. He had issued his celebrated proclamation of emancipation and immortalized himself by his Gettysburg address.

With the surrender of Lee, the Confederacy collapsed and the relief from the strain of four long years of war produced a marked revulsion of feeling toward Lincoln. People admire a winner.

"Nothing succeeds like success." Lincoln's modesty and tolerance in success also further endeared him to the people. His tragic death, occurring under such conditions, made him not only a national hero and martyr but also almost an object of worship. The same clergy who only a short time previously had vilified him now were loud in their praise of him, his sterling qualities and superb success. Of course, anyone of such a character and stature MUST BE A CHRISTIAN. He was claimed by the Methodists, Baptists, Presbyterians, Campbellites, and others.* Thousands of sermons were preached to prove him devoutly religious and credit his alleged prayers for his success in saving the nation. In fact, the hysterical efforts to prove Lincoln a saint exceeded in absurdity the hysteria four years earlier in the opposite direction.

Likewise his ancestral tarnish was rubbed from his escutcheon and the same polished until it glowed with a perpetual halo. His mother became second only to the Virgin Mary in her chastity. Volumes were written to prove the chastity of Nancy; all of these by people who had never known Nancy Hanks or who had never met anyone who had known her. (Nancy Hanks had died more than half a century before this.) This absence of historical perspective, however, has had little bearing upon the mental contortions of these hero worshippers.

Up to the time of Lincoln's death, there existed no authentic biography of the national hero. There

---

* A Psychic journal of February 10, 1943 claims Lincoln was a Spiritualist and it is also said he is claimed by the Mormons.

was, therefore, a rush to supply this want, for the first one out would mean a fortune to the lucky publisher. The first (and worst) biography to fill this want was a substantial volume by J. G. Holland, a man of unusual literary ability and possessed of a convenient conscience. A few troublesome historical facts were not allowed to interfere with the production of a "good" biography. He carefully avoided the annoying question of illegitimacy of Lincoln and his mother, though in his hasty investigations of Lincoln's early life, he was furnished an abundance of information along this line, as he also was in regard to Lincoln's lack of religious belief. On the latter, he not only ignored the matter, as in the case of Lincoln's ancestry, but indulged in the most outrageous mendacity in his attempts to misrepresent his hero as an extremely religious man and *boy*. Strangely, he neglects having Lincoln unite with any church.

Dr. Holland also overlooked the religious element entering into Lincoln's campaign for Congress, though he calls attention to the fact that Lincoln ran far ahead of his ticket in the election, but is strangely silent in regard to his notable opponent (the evangelist Cartwright), and this opponent's line of attack.

The lengths to which Holland goes in his attempts to make Lincoln a religious individual are so absurd as to make the book ridiculous—almost ludicrous. He says, "Both father and mother of Lincoln were religious persons, and sought at the earliest moment to impress the minds of their children with religious truth." How does Dr. Holland know this? He should tell us. He hasn't a shred of evidence for such a statement.

Holland further states:

"He (Lincoln) believed in his inmost soul that he was an instrument in the hands of God for the accomplishment of a great purpose." (This long before he became president.)* Again no evidence, for

---

*Recent light on this point is evidenced by the following by Henry Villard:

"The train that we intended to take for Springfield was about due. After vainly waiting for half an hour for its arrival, a thunderstorm compelled us to take refuge in an empty freight-car standing on a side track, there being no buildings of any sort at the station. We squatted down on the floor of the car and fell to talking on all sorts of subjects. It was then and there he told me that, when he was clerking in a country store, his highest political ambition was to be a member of the State Legislature. 'Since then, of course,' he said laughingly, 'I have grown some, but my friends got me into this business [meaning the canvass]. I did not consider myself qualified for the United States Senate, and it took me a long time to persuade myself that I was. Now to be sure,' he continued, with another of his peculiar laughs, 'I am convinced that I am good enough for it; but, in spite of it all, I am saying to myself every day: "It is too big a thing for you; you will never get it." Mary insists, however, that I am going to be Senator and President of the United States, too.' These last words he followed with a roar of laughter, with his arms around his knees, and shaking all over with mirth at his wife's ambition. 'Just think,' he exclaimed, 'of such a sucker as me as President!'

"He then fell to asking questions regarding my antecedents, and expressed some surprise at my fluent use of English after so short a residence in the United States. Next he wanted to know whether it was true that most of the educated people in Germany were 'infidels.' I answered that they were not openly professed infidels, but such a conclusion might be drawn from the fact that most of them were not church-goers. 'I do not wonder at that,' he rejoined; 'my own inclination is that way.' I ventured to give expression of my own disbelief in the doctrine of the Christian church relative to the existence of God, the divinity of Christ, and immortality. This led him to put other questions to me to draw me out. He did not commit himself, but I received the impression that he was of my own way of thinking. It was no surprise to me, therefore, to find in the writings of his biographers Ward Hill Lamon and W. H. Herndon that I had correctly understood him."

"Lincoln On the Eve of '61", published by
Alfred A. Knoph, New York, 1941.

Holland was not personally acquainted with Lincoln and there is not of record anywhere a statement of Lincoln which would indicate that he ever entertained any ideas remotely approaching anything so absurd as this.

"He (Lincoln) was in the White House as God's instrument." Doubtless God so informed Holland.

"It was one of the peculiarities of Mr. Lincoln to hide these religious experiences from the eyes of the world." How strange in a *politician* to do such a thing.   He also hid them from his most intimate friend and law partner, likewise hid them from his wife, his private secretary and his chief of staff, but, *after his death,* he proceeded to reveal them to Dr. Holland, whom he had never known. "Queer world!"

Perhaps the most damnable passage in Holland's entire book and the most damaging to his veracity, is his account of an interview with Newton Bateman, who was at the time State Superintendent of Public Instruction of Illinois, with an office in the same suite partly occupied by Lincoln. In this connection, it must be borne in mind that Bateman himself was exceedingly pious and orthodox. He, therefore, made as good a case for religion as possible in relating the interview he had with Lincoln on the matter of failure of the Christian ministers and other prominent Christians of Springfield to support Lincoln for president. Even in spite of this, after Holland's book was published, Bateman publicly stated that Holland had colored what he (Bateman) told in regard to Lincoln's attitude on religion. Holland, in his zeal to make a case for religion, became exceedingly careless, his own statements being contradictory.   According to Bateman's statement, Lincoln opened the interview

with, "Mr. Bateman, I am not a Christian . . . .
LINCOLN OUGHT TO KNOW.

In this connection, I, perhaps, may be pardoned
for a personal experience. I also had a slight ac-
quaintance with Dr. Bateman, who was president
emeritus of Knox College when I entered the school
in the nineties. Just previously I had picked up
somewhere the rumor that Lincoln wasn't a
Christian, and I was duly horrified and troubled
over the matter, for like most young Americans,
I was taught to worship Lincoln next to God.

One day an errand took me to the residence of
Dr. Bateman. He himself answered the doorbell,
invited me in, and, as he did so, directed me to
hang my cap upon a certain peg in a small walnut
hat-tree which stood in his hallway. After I had
done this, he said, "Now, young man, you can state
that you have hung your cap upon the same peg
upon which Abraham Lincoln hung his hat for
many years." As a youngster, I was, of course,
duly thrilled, and, forgetting the purpose of my
errand for the time, I proceeded to ply the good
doctor with questions about Lincoln, with whom I
knew he had been acquainted.

I therefore, at an opportune moment, said to
Mr. Bateman: "Someone has told me that Mr. Lincoln was not a Christian. You must know. Is there
anything to this report?" The old gentleman laid
his hand on my shoulder and replied, "My young
friend, the less said about that, the better."

As I left Dr. Bateman I was greatly troubled,
for fully realizing that his answer meant that
Lincoln really was not a Christian, I proceeded to
investigate. The investigation revealed much to
me in regard to the beliefs, or *lack of beliefs*, of
eminent men. Much later, after a perusal of the
extensive literature of Lincoln, I also realize that

Dr. Bateman may have been saving himself embarrassment on account of his own over zealous interview with Holland.

Edgar Lee Masters, author of "Lincoln the Man," said of this Bateman interview with Holland, "Such words do not sound honest, sensible, coming from the Lincoln that we know."

Dr. Holland, also, completely ignored the much discussed question of Lincoln's ancestry. That this avoidance of the question was deliberate, Herndon's notes and letters now reveal. In fact, Holland, in his preface, acknowledges his obligation to Herndon — Lincoln's law partner — though he apparently profited little by the information furnished by Herndon, writing what he thought Lincoln should have been rather than what he was, for Herndon made it very plain to Holland that Lincoln was very unorthodox in his religious beliefs.

Holland also completely ignored Lincoln's romance with Ann Rutledge. This is of especial interest, for at the time Holland gathered his data (1865) there must have lived a number of people who had known both Ann Rutledge and Lincoln.

*    *    *

I have dwelt at some length upon Holland's shortcomings, because he was a literary man of some prestige and influence. His book, also, is the first on the Civil War President, is quite pretentious, 600 pages, and the first edition was bound like a bible — whether this was because of the amount of religion Holland injected into it or the amount of fiction contained in it is not now possible to know. However, because of its priority, its literary merit (for it has *literary* merit), its pretentious appearance and the standing of the author, the book greatly influenced a large number of later biographers, with the result that Lincoln's "piety" grew like the proverbial snowball rolling down hill, finally reaching somewhat of a climax in a volume from the pen of one John Wesley (sic) Hill, D.D., entitled, "Abraham Lincoln, Man of God" (though what God is not stated). This rare gem was given to the world in 1920 with an introduction by the late Warren G. Harding, who says:

"Abraham Lincoln was born amid a somewhat primitive and tumultuous religious upheaval expressed in the powerful preaching of Peter Cartwright and illustrated in the perennial popularity of the camp-meeting. Brought up by parents whose lives were lived amid such influences, Abraham Lincoln was from his earliest years religious. The Bible was the book of books to him. He prayed so constantly and so confidently as to seem a kind of modern Brother Lawrence practicing the Presence of God. He worked out a theology in general conformity with the accepted standards of Christianity. In the darkest hour of his White House days when personal bereavement was added to national anxiety, he literally lived on his knees." This, therefore, becomes authoritative; in fact, uttered as it was in October, 1920, it doubtless was *inspired*. This volume claims that, while president, Lincoln spent much of his time "on his knees in prayer." It likewise demonstrates that his prayers were answered. It quotes from one Mrs. Pomeroy (page 282) an account of her calling upon President Lincoln during the battle of Port Hudson and finding the president greatly depressed and worried over the outcome of the battle, she advised him to pray, which he did, and a few minutes after the prayer, a sentinel appeared with a telegram from the front, announcing a victory for the Union arms, thus greatly relieving Lincoln. That at least several hours were required to get such a message on the wires, transmitted to Washington and delivered to the president, also that the action for the reduction of Port Hudson commenced on December 14th and lasted until July 8th of the following year, makes one entitled to consider the answer to Lincoln's prayer as theologically ex post facto.

One other demonstration from Rev. Hill; during the battle of Gettysburg, someone reported Lincoln to have said:

"I went to my room one day and locked the door and got down on my knees before Almighty God and prayed to Him mightily for victory at Gettysburg. I told Him that this war was His, and our cause His cause, but we could not stand another Fredericksburg or Chancellorsville. Then and there I made a solemn vow to Almighty God that if He would stand by our boys at Gettysburg, I would stand by Him."* (Can one imagine Lincoln making such a statement?)

Then Rev. Hill describes the battle thus:

"The Confederacy reached its high-water mark at Gettysburg. The battle started by mistake, and the charge of the First Minnesota Regiment, with its resultant losses, broke the record of the Civil War for fatality. Pickett's charge and repulse reached the bloody angle of pre-eminence. At sundown, General Meade was bewildered, not knowing what step to take next, when a strange and irresistible impression moved him to order up his reserves. At daylight, he was ready to meet the Confederate advance. He had a similar experience the second night with a similar result."

---

* Similar to the story of "Me und Got" attributed to Kaiser Wilhelm.

That a "strange and irresistible impression" should "move a general to order up his reserves," at a critical time is indeed remarkable! One is also tempted to wonder why the God of battle did not have General Meade blow the Confederates off the field with a ram's horn as did his General Joshua at Jericho. This would have saved the slaughter of many thousands of reserves. One is also inclined to wonder just why God did not recognize the devout prayers of General Lee in this same battle, for Lee was supposed to have much greater influence with the Almighty, as Lee had all his life been a praying man, while Lincoln never used this technique until he got into the White House and then only on authority of the clerics.

In this volume of over 400 pages, God appears on very many of the pages. This is doubtless the same God who directed Joshua in the massacre of the entire population of Jericho (except one harlot and her kin); the same God who guided the hand of General Moses in the slaughter of all the Midianites (except 32,000 virgins who were turned over to the sport of the soldiers of God); the same God who directed his favorite, the bastard Jephthah, in the sack and slaughter of twenty cities of the Ammonites (then showed his appreciation of Jephthah by requiring him to burn his daughter alive). It was doubtless the same bloodthirsty god.

Pennell also published (1899) a pamphlet attempting to prove Lincoln religious. His effort is noteworthy chiefly for its omissions and its extremely evangelistic tone. Lincoln was selected by providence to free the slaves and save the union. He, by means of his prayers, won the battles of Gettysburg and Vicksburg, this in spite of the fact that Lincoln gave the infidel General Grant credit for the latter victory. Pennell admits that the

boyhood of Lincoln "was not characterized by anything supernatural," though claims "his face had
a Christ-like appearance." Inasmuch as the writer
has not seen Christ, it is not possible to take ex-
ception to this comparison. Pennell also offers another proof of Lincoln's religious belief to the effect
that the emancipated negroes, whenever assembled
for worship, always gave thanks to God for their
emancipator. It never seemed to have occurred to
him that the same God was responsible for placing
the negroes in bondage. In fact, had he chosen to
investigate the history of human slavery in
America, he would have been edified by the discov-
ery that a Christian priest by the name of Las
Casas, in the sixteenth century was the first to
suggest that African Negroes be imported to work
the plantations — thus initiating our American
slave trade.

The evangelistic Pennell finds only one defect in
the long holy life of Lincoln—he chose a theatre
in which to die which, Pennell "would have ordered
otherwise." To the ungodly it also seems strange
that God would choose Lincoln to do this great
work, then, when he was in the very midst of it,
decoy him into an unholy place and cause or at
least permit him to be assassinated.

Sandburg, in his comprehensive work ("Abraham Lincoln—The War Years"; V. III, p. 378),
relates several accounts by Mrs. Pomeroy, Dan
Sickles, and others, of Lincoln's praying. Sandburg
then says, "Were these accounts of Lincoln as a
praying man strictly accurate? It is rather likely
they were not . . . . Nicolay and Hay, Stoddard,
Carpenter, Chaplain Neill, the guard Crook, these
White House residents, with far better opportuni-
ties for observation, left no record of having seen

nor reliably heard from the President or anyone else of his having thus invoked the Lord."

Sandburg also states Lincoln was once (while president) asked as to his conception of God and replied that it was the same as his conception of nature.

Now, it is not so important whether Lincoln may have indulged in an occasional prayer after he became president, though there is no reliable evidence that he ever did. The really interesting feature of this religious hysteria concerning Lincoln is, that *previous to his nomination for the presidency, he was roundly condemned by the clergy as an infidel, while after his martyrdom, the same clerics were loud in their claims of his piety*—not alone his piety after becoming president, but many of them claimed he was pious in youth and of pious parents, though not one of these writers ever knew his parents or knew Lincoln in his youth. (Yet when he was a candidate for president, only three of the 23 ministers of his own community supported him.) Many of these writers were so bent upon making a saint of Lincoln that they not only suppressed important facts of Lincoln's life, but frequently indulged in outright mendacity of the most outrageous character. It is but fair in passing to note that the more sane biographers of Lincoln, especially those biographers who were acquainted with him, have a decidedly different opinion of Lincoln's piety or lack of it. Herndon, Lincoln's most intimate friend and law partner for a quarter of a century, the man with whom he advised, not only in law, but in all political and many private and personal matters, is most emphatic in his statements that Lincoln was highly unorthodox if not actually irreligious. *Who would know of this better than Herndon?* It might also be noted that Herndon was noted for his honesty and

candor.   He was a man who was honest, not because it was a good policy, but was one of those
rather rare individuals who had an honest mind,
a mind which could not tolerate a falsehood, regardless of its effect.   In his biography, he took a
scientific attitude toward matters of historical im-
port—the *truth*, the *whole truth*, must be told at all
costs.   Furthermore, most of the written record of
Lincoln left by Herndon was prepared for the purpose of lectures and much was thus used before
Illinois audiences shortly after Lincoln's death.
Therefore thousands of people who had seen and
heard Lincoln and hundreds who knew him intimately were in a position to correct any errors
which Herndon made or any wrong conclusions at
which he arrived.

Then there is Colonel Lamon, probably the most
confidential of Lincoln's official family, a man who
greatly loved Lincoln, and was most intimately
associated with him during the last four years of
his life, and who also states that Lincoln was an
infidel; not only states it to be a fact, but marshals
a formidable array of evidence to prove the statement. Lamon quotes from a large number of
friends and relatives of Lincoln who furnish comprehensive and overwhelming evidence that Lincoln was not only unorthodox, but in reality an infidel.

Lamon, (p. 276) says with reference to Lincoln's
candidacy for Congress: "He was called a deist and
an infidel, both before and after his nomination,
and encountered in a less degree the same opposition from the members of certain religious
bodies that had met him before."

Few people are in a better position to know of
the personal beliefs of a man than his private
secretary. Lincoln's private secretary for the entire

time he was president was John G. Nicolay, who, in a letter dated May 27, 1865, states: "Mr. Lincoln did not, to my knowledge, in any way, change his religious ideas, opinions or beliefs from the time he left Springfield till the day of his death." Nicolay knew Lincoln in Springfield, accompanied him on his memorable trip to Washington, and was his private secretary until Lincoln's death.

One of Lincoln's most intimate associates was Judge David Davis, before whose bench Lincoln practiced for many years, who managed the campaign which made Lincoln president and who was later appointed to the Supreme Court of the United States by Lincoln. Judge Davis has stated for publication, "He (Lincoln) had no faith, in the Christian sense of the term — had faith in laws, principles, causes, and effects — philosophically."

It might be presumed that Lincoln's wife might know something of his beliefs. She states (also for publication): "Mr. Lincoln had no hope, and no faith, in the usual acceptation of those words."

John E. Remsburg, in his volume, "Six Historic Americans" has carefully compiled and admirably organized the evidence pro and con on Lincoln's religious, or lack of religious views. A perusal of this work can leave no doubt in any honest and rational mind that Lincoln was highly unorthodox —in fact probably an infidel.

With reference to the allegation that Lincoln, in his later years, became religious, the New York World a number of years ago may have furnished the correct explanation. In an editorial it said: "While it may fairly be said that Mr. Lincoln entertained many Christian sentiments, it cannot be said that he was himself a Christian in faith or practice. He was no disciple of Jesus of Nazareth.

He did not believe in his divinity and was not a member of his church.

"He was at first a writing Infidel of the school of Paine and Volney, and afterward a talking Infidel of the school of Parker and Channing."

Alluding to the friendly attitude he assumed toward the church and Christianity during the war, this article concludes:

"If the churches had grown cold — if the Christians had taken a stand aloof — that instant the Union would have perished. Mr. Lincoln regulated his religious manifestations accordingly. He declared frequently that he would do *anything* to save the Union, and among the many things he did was the partial concealment of his individual religious opinions. Is this a blot upon his fame? Or shall we all agree that it was a conscientious and patriotic sacrifice?"

To quote from Remsburg, "Manford's Magazine, a *religious* periodical published in Chicago, in its issue for January, 1869, contained the following:

" 'That Mr. Lincoln was a believer in the Christian religion, as understood by the so-called orthodox sects of the day, I am compelled most emphatically to deny; that is, if I put faith in the statements of his most intimate friends in this city (Springfield). All of them with whom I have conversed on this subject agree in indorsing the statements of Mr. Herndon. Indeed, many of them unreservedly call him an Infidel.'

" 'The evidence on this subject is sufficient, the writer says, to place the name of Lincoln by the side of Franklin, Washington, Jefferson, and (Ethan) Allen, of Revolutionary notoriety, as Rationalists; besides being in company with D'Alembert, the great mathematician, Diderot, the geometrician, poet, and meta-physician; also with Voltaire, Hume, Gibbon, and Darwin.'

"Referring to the Infidel book, written by Lincoln, the writer says:

" 'This work was subsequently thrown in Mr. Lincoln's face while he was stumping this district for Congress against the celebrated Methodist preacher, Rev. Peter Cartwright. But Mr. Lincoln never publicly or privately denied its authorship, or the sentiments expressed therein. Nor was he known to change his religious views any, to the latest period of his life.'

"The article concludes with these truthful words:

" 'Mr. Lincoln was too good a man to be a Pharisee; too great a man to be a sectarian; and too charitable a man to be a bigot.'

"This work, in an abridged form, originally appeared in the Truth Seeker in 1889 and 1890. After its appearance, the Adventist Herald and Review, one of the fairest and most ably conducted religious journals in this country, said:

" 'The Truth Seeker has just concluded the publication of a series of fifteen contributed articles designed to prove that Abraham Lincoln, instead of being a Christian, as has been most strongly claimed by some, was a Freethinker. The testimony seems conclusive. . . . The majority of the great men of the world have always rejected Christ, and, according to the Scriptures, they always will; and the efforts of Christians to make it appear that certain great men who never professed Christianity were in reality Christians, is simply saying that Christianity cannot stand on its merits, but must have the support of great names to entitle it to favorable consideration.' "

One might quote a large number of persons who knew Lincoln with reference to his unorthodox views, but the evidence would only be cumulative and unnecessary. However, two members of Lincoln's family should be noted.  Katherine Helm, a niece of Mrs. Lincoln, in her book "Mary, Wife of Lincoln," makes no mention of Lincoln's piety, which is significant in view of the fact that she was acquainted with Lincoln and her book deals with the more intimate and personal matters of the Lincoln Family.

The other is John T. Stuart, a cousin of Mrs. Lincoln and Lincoln's first law partner.  Stuart states that Lincoln "was an open infidel" and while he was associated with him never regularly attended any church.

Elizabeth Keckley, a servant of Mrs. Lincoln while in the White House, wrote in some detail her experiences in the Lincoln Family ("Behind the Scenes"). She refers several times to the prayers of Mrs. Lincoln, but never once to any religious formalities or prayers by the president.

Walt Whitman, who was acquainted with Lincoln, makes this rather significant statement, "I shouldn't wonder but that in another age of the world, Lincoln would have been a chosen man to lead in some rebellion against ecclesiastical institutions and religious forms and ceremony."

Before leaving this topic it will be interesting to note a statement by Rev. A. T. Goodloe, M.D., an ex-Confederate officer who served throughout the war. Goodloe kept a diary recording events connected with Lincoln's election and other incidents until well into the reconstruction period. From this diary he has written a book entitled "Confederate Echoes," published in 1907 by the M. E. Church South. Of Lincoln, Goodloe states:

"But it is a fact that he was not known to have professed in any presence to be a Christian, nor evinced any real interest in religion; on the other hand, he was known to have shown contempt for the whole system of Christianity and its divine Founder, and at one time to have written a book against them. By profession he had been an infidel and religious scoffer. . . . .

"Notwithstanding these facts, his admiring biographers and apologists have written voluminously to show up in a bright light his Christian character, as they would have it. Nothing of this sort was thought of before Booth shot him, but ever since then they have been on the hunt for some sure evidence that he was a Christian. No such evidence has been found, and there is no likelihood that it ever will be. Indeed, if he had been a Christian, the evidence of it, in the position he occupied, would have been before the world, and not to be hunted up, as it has been, without the slightest likelihood of finding it. Was it ever so before, that searchers without number must be sent out in every direction to find the proof that a man was a Christian?"

Edward Bates, Attorney General in Lincoln's cabinet, and an intimate of Lincoln, kept a very detailed diary, for the period 1859-1866 inclusive, in which he records many incidents in regard to Lincoln, and members of Lincoln's family, including the death of Willie Lincoln, but not a word does he say in regard to any Lincoln prayers or piety. It should be noted that Mr. Bates was himself quite religious.

A quotation from Remsburg's "Six Historic Americans" is interesting in this connection:

"It is difficult for orthodox Christians to reconcile Lincoln's fondness for the play with his re-

puted piety. That his last act was a visit to the
theatre is a fact that stands out in ghastly prominence to them.    To break its force they offer
various explanations.    Some say that he went to
avoid the office-seekers; others that Mrs. Lincoln
compelled him to go; and still others that he was
led there by fate. The truth is he was a frequent
attendant at the theater.   He went there much
oftener than he went to church.   The visit of a
clergyman annoyed him, but the society of actors
he enjoyed. He greatly admired the acting of Edwin Booth. He sent a note to the actor Hackett,
praising him for his fine presentation of Falstaff.
He called John McCulloch to his box one night and
congratulated him on his successful rendition of
the part he was playing.

"In his autobiography, which recently appeared
in the Century Magazine, Joseph Jefferson gives
some interesting reminiscences of Lincoln. In the
earlier part of his dramatic career, he was connected with a theatrical company, the managers of
which, one of whom was his father, built a theater
in Springfield, Ill. A conflict between the preachers
and players ensued. The church was powerful then,
and the city joined with the church to suppress the
theater. The history of the struggle and its term-
ination, as narrated by Mr. Jefferson, is as follows:

" 'In the midst of their rising fortunes a heavy
blow fell upon them.  A religious revival was in
progress at the time, and the fathers of the church
not only launched forth against us in their sermons, but by some political maneuver got the city
to pass a new law enjoining a heavy license against
our "unholy" calling; I forget the amount, but it
was large enough to be prohibitory. Here was a
terrible condition of affairs — all our available
funds invested, the Legislature in session, the town

full of people, and by a heavy license denied the privilege of opening the new theater!

" 'In the midst of their trouble a young lawyer called on the managers. He had heard of the injustice, and offered, if they would place the matter in his hands, to have the license taken off, declaring that he only desired to see fair play, and he would accept no fcc whether he failed or succeeded. The case was brought up before the council. The young man began his harangue. He handled the subject with tact, skill, and humor, tracing the history of the drama from the time when Thespis acted in a cart to the stage of to-day. He illustrated his speech with a number of anecdotes, and kept the council in a roar of laughter; his good humor prevailed, and the exorbitant tax was taken off.

" 'This young lawyer was very popular in Springfield, and was honored and beloved by all who knew him, and, after the time of which I write, he held rather an important position in the Government of the United States. He now lies buried near Springfield, under a monument commemorating his greatness and his virtues—and his name was Abraham Lincoln.' "

\*     \*     \*

A story is told in regard to President Eliot of Harvard, who, at the time, was the youngest college president in the country. Someone congratulated Eliot's uncle upon the nephew's appointment to the exalted position. The uncle shook his head dubiously and stated that it had been his observation that soon after a man became a college president he usually became an awful liar.

Some allowance, therefore, must be made for the usual man in public office, especially if he is politically ambitious. He may be a man of high ideals, but he will frequently be tempted to rationalize himself around these troublesome ideals and along the lines of least resistance. An observation of Lincoln himself along this line may be of interest: "Politicians who have interests aside from the interest of the people, are—that is, the most of them are—at least one long step removed from honest men. I say this with greater freedom because, being a politician myself, none can regard it as personal." Thus Lincoln frequently found it expedient to allow certain religious fanatics in his cabinet and elsewhere to have their way in injecting God into public documents and otherwise making it appear that Lincoln was guilty of making these cheap religious gestures. These acts, and the publicity given to them by religious propagandists, led many people to think Lincoln had undergone a change in his religious views and stimulated Judge J. A. Wakefield, a long time religious friend, to write Lincoln and express the hope that he had become a Christian. Lincoln replied by letter in 1862, saying, "My earlier views of the unsoundness of the Christian scheme of salvation and the human origin of the scriptures have become clearer and stronger with advancing years, and I see no reason for thinking I shall ever change them."

Ida Tarbell, in her Life of Lincoln, (Volume I, page 206) says of the Lincoln-Cartwright campaign for Congress, "Cartwright now made an energetic canvass, his chief weapon against Lincoln being the old charges of atheism— —"

Also in Volume II, page 90, "Religion up to this time (i. e. death of Lincoln's son Willie) had been an intellectual interest," yet Miss Tarbell seems to think that later in life Christianity had some influence upon him, but says, "though there is nothing to show that Mr. Lincoln turned to the literal interpretation of Christianity . . . . . . and he never joined any religious sect." It might be added that Miss Tarbell was, herself, very religious, and also has done a tremendous amount of investigation of Lincoln history.

It is a poor recommendation for a religion that a person only turns to it when emotionally upset over the loss of someone near and dear to him. If the religion is what its proponents claim for it, it should appeal to the reason and judgment of one in his calm and undisturbed moments when his mental faculties are at their best. According to the unctuous biographers it only appealed to Lincoln when he lost a son or thought he was about to lose an important battle.

It is also interesting to note that Lincoln's illustrious political opponent, Stephen A. Douglas, was likewise an unbeliever. A Boston newspaper, in publishing an account of his death, said:

"When Stephen A. Douglas lay stricken with death at Chicago, his wife, who was a devout Roman Catholic, sent for Bishop Duggan, who asked whether he had ever been baptized according to the rites of any church. 'Never,' replied Mr. Douglas. 'Do you desire to have mass said after the ordinances of the holy Catholic church?' inquired the Bishop. 'No, sir!' answered Douglas; 'when I do I will communicate with you freely.'

"The Bishop withdrew, but the next day Mrs. Douglas sent for him again, and, going to the bedside, he said: 'Mr. Douglas, you know your own condition fully, and in view of your dissolution do you desire the ceremony of extreme unction to be performed?' 'No!' replied the dying man, 'I have no time to discuss these things now.'

"The Bishop left the room, and Mr. Rhodes, who was in attendance, said: 'Do you know the clergymen of this city?' 'Nearly every one of them.' 'Do you wish to have either or any of them to call to see you to converse on religious topics?' 'No, I thank you,' was the decided answer."

There has been a deal of romancing by Lincoln biographers, and the end is not yet, for we find Sandburg (a recent biographer) saying with reference to Thomas Lincoln as a boy or young man, "Church meetings interested him. . . Sometimes he felt stirred inside when a young woman kneeling on the floor would turn a passionate, longing face to the roof of the cabin, and call, 'Jesus, I give everything to thee. I give thee all. I give thee all. I am wholly thine!'" Was this female near the microphone? Or was there a stenographic report? Does Sandburg know just what portion of Thomas Lincoln's "inside" was *stirred* by this fanatical female? Freud would say the *author* was probably "stirred" by the thought—of something.

Sandburg calls attention to the efforts of a clergyman to form a creed for Lincoln by changing pronouns in some of his references to the deity and prefixing the words "I believe." Sandburg then takes this fictitious and fanciful creed, makes further additions to it "in order to make it a liturgical expression of faith," and proceeds to formulate a creed of six or eight hundred words, all of which is pure fiction. Each of the twenty-three paragraphs of the creed commences with the expression "I believe," and has Lincoln "believing" in some of the most puerile, ridiculous things imaginable. This is not biography. It is not even good fiction, but fabrication or balderdash of the basest sort. Further, Sandburg must know that the clergy will be quick to lift this "creed" from his biography without reference to the context, or explanation that it is an imaginary creed. It probably has already been printed and circulated as "Lincoln's creed, formulated and written by Lincoln, himself, *when a boy, and used as his guide throughout life*," just as the clergy took a few statements from Washington's letter to the governors of the states, to which some religious expressions had been added by one of his secretaries, and from it forged "Washington's Prayer," which they had done into a bronze plate and placed on the wall of St. Paul's chapel on Broadway in New York City. Washington closed his letter as follows: "I have the honor to be, with much esteem and respect, sir, your Excellency's most obedient and humble servant." This sentence was changed by the ministers to read, "Grant our supplication, we beseech Thee, through Jesus Christ our Lord. Amen." A more outrageous and shameful case of forgery could scarcely be found. Fortunately, this bit of ecclesiastical mendacity has been exposed by the historians, Rupert Hughes and Franklin Steiner; however, the truths of these historical writers will never "catch up" with the Christian lie.

So with Sandburg's imaginary creed; it will furnish the necessary material for a never ending stream of propaganda with Lincoln as the innocent victim—aye! with innocent youth also victims of this vicious practice.

It is most astounding that a biographer would lift from Lincoln's Emancipation Proclamation the phrase "gracious favor of Almighty God," which admittedly was interpolated by Secretary Chase, and distort the same into "I believe in praise to Almighty God, the beneficent Creator and Ruler of the Universe." When a youth becomes disillusioned from reading such history and biography, have we a right to be surprised if his views are more or less Bolshevik?

One popular biography states in its opening paragraph that its purpose is "to portray the character of Abraham Lincoln as the highest type of the American." What can be expected from an author in such a frame of mind?

Several "lives of Lincoln" state at the outset that Lincoln was appointed by divine providence to do the work he did, while one scribe states that it is reported on good authority (though he does not state what authority) that a "faint halo or glow" could be seen about him as a young child. The author does not explain why the halo was "faint," or why confined to childhood.

Ida Tarbell says, "His father was illiterate, unable to sign his name save with difficulty, and never known to read any book but the Bible." How could an illiterate person read anything, especially the Bible, one of the most difficult of books to read? Such a statement surely exposes the mental and moral state of its author.

The mental condition of such writers is a sad commentary on our twentieth century civilization and the fact that publishers will dispense such nonsense to the public a serious reflection upon twentieth century morality.

Lincoln relates that when the Universalists attempted to effect an organization in Springfield, the orthodox clergy agreed to each preach against the new cult. One of these preachers said, "My Brethren, there is a dangerous doctrine creeping in among us. There are those who are teaching that all men will be saved; but my dear brethren, *we* hope for better things."

This question of Lincoln's religion has been dwelt upon at some length as it is this feature of Lincoln which has suffered most abuse by the "biographers" and birthday orators.

Probably the most significant environmental factor influencing the mental evolution of Lincoln was William Herndon, for over twenty years Lincoln's law partner. Herndon was a likeable fellow and greatly admired Lincoln. Lincoln, in turn, had the utmost confidence in Herndon. Herndon was a student—a student more of philosophy than of law. His library on philosophical and scientific subjects was one of the best in the west. He kept abreast of the latest and best thought of the scholars of the day—read Origin of Species as soon as it was off the press. Not only read, but appreciated it. He was not only an inveterate reader, but a man of energy and force. His knowledge, therefore, was translated into action and his intellectual influence was felt among his associates. Lincoln, who was not much of a reader, absorbed much from Herndon to whom he constantly turned for advice upon intellectual matters.

Several students who read law in the office of Lincoln and Herndon throw much light upon this question. J. H. Littlefield, one of these students, says, "Outside of his law-tomes, I never noticed that Lincoln was much of a reader. . . . . Strange to say, the man who was destined within five years to liberate millions of negroes by a stroke of his pen, was not nearly so fervid an Abolitionist as his partner." Charles Zane, whom Herndon advised "to keep out of politics until he had a practice, and then stay out in order to keep it," says Herndon "was a rapid thinker, writer and speaker, and usually reached his conclusions quickly and expressed them forcibly and positively. . . . He never harbored ill will or malice toward any man, and if he ever had an enemy, I never knew it." H. B. Rankin states that often Lincoln would stretch himself on the office cot and say, "Now, Billy, tell

me about the books," while Herndon would discourse by the hour upon philosophy and science.
These students state that Herndon constantly en-
deavored to interest those about him in matters of
general culture.

Lincoln in a letter to Herndon (7/10/48) makes
this significant statement, "You (i. e. Herndon)
are far better informed on almost all subjects than
I have ever been."

Nor was Herndon's influence confined to the education of Lincoln. He, with his fiery zeal and immense energy, interested many of the anti-slavery
leaders in Lincoln, not least among these Theodore
Parker and Horace Greeley, both of whom wielded
tremendous influence.

Perhaps one reason for our over admiration of
Lincoln was Herndon's almost worshipful admiration of him; yet Herndon could see his faults.

"I know Lincoln better than he knows himself.
I know this seems a little strong, but I risk the as-
sertion. Lincoln is a man of heart—aye, as gentle
as a woman's and as tender — but he has a will
strong as iron. He therefore loves all mankind,
hates slavery and every form of despotism. . . . . .
If any question comes up which is doubtful, ques-
tionable, which no man can demonstrate, then his
friends can rule him; but when on Justice, Right,
Liberty, the Government, the Constitution, and the
Union . . . . . . he will rule them and no man can
move him." (W. H. Herndon in letter to Hon.
Henry Wilson, December 21, 1860.)

Some day historians will accord to Herndon the
credit due him for his immense influence over Lincoln, for his contributions in moulding the early
Republican policies and his influence in anti-slavery
matters.

As previously stated, one of the important factors in Lincoln's mental development was the Lincoln-Douglas debates. Lincoln, more or less deficient in formal education and some of the refinements of society, also with a brain rather slow to act, met in mental contest an educated, sophisticated, clever, skilled, and experienced debater. Lincoln, an obscure country lawyer, met a statesman of ability and reputation who had the political advantage of having been persecuted by an unpopular administration. For Lincoln to challenge Douglas to debate under such circumstances required no small amount of courage, though, of course, Lincoln had everything to gain and little to lose by such an encounter.

The debates were a stimulus to marked intellectual growth on the part of Lincoln, whose ability as a debater increased from the beginning. Lincoln's courage was bolstered by his zeal in a great moral issue—human slavery—and his political ambition. His intense interest in the rights of man, together with his ability to present the matter in a manner appreciated by the people of the day, enabled Lincoln to win the popular verdict, notwithstanding Douglas' greater ability as a debater.

The debates, likewise, brought Lincoln into national prominence and made him one of the leaders of the anti-slavery forces.

Herndon's letters written to Parker at the time of the debates furnish one of the best historical accounts of the Lincoln-Douglas campaign.

Though receiving a majority of the popular votes in the election, Lincoln failed to secure a majority of the legislators and Douglas was elected senator. Lincoln accepted his defeat as final and said, "I am glad I made the race, and though I now sink out of view, I believe I have made some marks which will tell for the cause of civil liberty long after I am gone."

Another important feature in Lincoln's education—for his was a mentality which was capable of education throughout life—was the above mentioned Theodore Parker. Parker was a Unitarian preacher who was too liberal even for this cult. He rejected all of the orthodox views of Christianity and was frequently denounced as an infidel. With his own congregations he was, however, influential and popular—his congregations in Boston seldom being less than 3,000. Parker entered into the anti-slavery movement with the zeal of a crusader, speaking and writing incessantly, in the cause of freedom and the natural rights of man. In fact he was said to have surpassed Lovejoy in influence, on account of his greater ability and wisdom. He also was active in aiding the escape of slaves. He lectured widely throughout the North, in 1856 lecturing in Springfield, Illinois. Herndon and Parker kept up a lively correspondence for a number of years, and Parker's influence upon the opinions and enthusiasm of Herndon was pronounced—all of which likewise had its effect upon Lincoln. Lincoln was once asked as to his religious views and replied that they were essentially those of Theodore Parker.

It can safely be asserted that the influence of the intellectual and dynamic Parker had much to do in moulding the thought and action of Lincoln on the question of slavery and democracy. The Historian Louis A. Warren says, "Five years before Gettysburg, Lincoln acquired two pamphlets containing addresses by Theodore Parker, delivered in 1858. In one of Parker's speeches, Lincoln underlined this statement: 'Democracy—The All Man Power; government over all, by all, and for the sake of all.'

The other pamphlet contained a sermon delivered by Parker in Music Hall, Boston, on July 4, 1858, and these words Lincoln enclosed with a pencil: 'Democracy is Direct Self-Government over all the people, for all the people, by all the people.'"

\* \* \*

It is really a tragedy that the two national characters whose birthdays we celebrate should be made to appear so ridiculous. Much educational good might be accomplished by a study and consideration of these men as they *were* rather than of some fantastic and ridiculous image created to satisfy the whim of priest or politician.

As men they were not superior to Franklin or Jefferson; nor were their public careers any more illustrious or valuable to the country. Yet of the latter, the average person takes a sane and sensible view. From their lives and activities we derive untold educational value. Whereas, of Lincoln and Washington, we derive little or nothing, as we rarely are able to get behind the fictitious and fantastic image to catch a glimpse of the real man.

The average clerics are unable to make a public address without indulging in religious propaganda. They do this unconsciously and often with no ulterior motive. Religious propaganda is their business, or profession, if it may be so dignified. In their social palaver, they are always "blessing," or "god blessing" or in some other manner ringing the changes on their moribund theology. They are, likewise, greatly addicted to hyperbole, to put it mildly. Therefore, if called upon to talk about an historical character, they unconsciously carry over their evangelistic habits with the result, an apotheosis rather than a scientific consideration of the character in question. From this, the invariable corollary follows — the individual, if good and great, is perforce a devout Christian, and they reiterate the statement so often that they themselves sooner or later come to believe it, and eventually the unthinking public also believes it.

There are over 70,000 cities and towns in the United States. At least 50,000 of them will have Lincoln birthday celebrations each year—some of the larger cities holding a number of these celebrations. It is therefore not improbable that every year there is perpetrated upon the defenseless, gullible and uninformed public, a torrent of tommy-rot from 25,000 to 50,000 evangelistic preachers—99.9% of whom emphasize Lincoln's piety. Just reflect on the score or more panegyrics you have heard on Lincoln and see if any of them failed to emphasize his religion.* Washington has suffered in the same manner. He also was a freethinker and not a communicant of any church, yet Parson Weems' fable of Washington's praying at Valley Forge is the one salient feature which stands out in all Washington birthday celebrations. A few days since, a local superintendent of schools was exhibiting some of his High School students before a Rotary Club; one young man making a speech on "patriotism." This pupil stated that one of the

---

* After this copy had gone to the publisher, the author was privileged to attend another Lincoln birthday celebration, an evening banquet open to the public. The inspirational talent consisted of three lawyers and a cleric. The barrister toastmaster informed us that "We admired Lincoln on account of his Christian background and Christian principles." The orator of the occasion, a State Supreme Court Justice, and a man old enough to have been acquainted with a good many people who knew Lincoln, said, "When I was a boy, we saw nothing unusual in Lincoln. Now we know he cannot be explained except upon divine intercession." A telegram was read from the governor of the state. He managed to link God with Lincoln four times in a short message.

chief ways the school taught patriotism was by calling attention to Washington's prayer at Valley Forge. This statement evidently had the approval of the school authorities. It is also more than probable that said school authorities likewise knew they were prostituting the good name of Washington and the innocence of youth for religious purposes. Could anything be more base?

The inconsistency of putting forth such an amount of labor and energy to make Washington and Lincoln appear religious, when most of the early founders of our republic were freethinkers and infidels, makes the case against the clergy and hypocritical biographers all the more impressive. We are, in fact, greatly indebted to a group of illustrious freethinkers for our democracy and human liberty today—Jefferson, Paine, Franklin, Adams, Gallatin, Monroe, Marshall, Mason. These and others of like belief (perhaps more correctly unbelief), nursed the young republic through its infancy and formulated its constitution—with god definitely voted out of it, and prayers emphatically proscribed from the deliberations of the constitutional convention. In fact, the clergy of the time were virtually all Tories. Then, too, the nation seemed to follow the lead of the non-religious founders, for it did not, for the next hundred years —from Washington to Garfield—elect to the presidency, a communicant of any orthodox church.

Further these two national idols (Washington and Lincoln) whom the clergy and the hypocrites would make saints, in their official actions, proceeded along anything but religious lines; Washington appointing as his secretary of state, Thomas Jefferson—one of the most outspoken infidels of the time, and who said of the Christian religion:

"I have recently been examining all the known

superstitutions of the world, and do not find in our particular superstitution (Christianity) one redeeming feature. They are all alike, founded upon fables and mythologies."

"We discover (in the four Gospels) a groundwork of vulgar ignorance, of things impossible, of superstitution, fanaticism and fabrication."

"It is wicked and tyrannical to compel any man to support a religion in which he does not believe."

"The day will come when the mystical generation of Jesus by the Supreme Being will be classed with the fable of the generation of Minerva in the brain of Jupiter."

"Calvin's religion was demonism. If ever a man worshipped a false god, he did. The God (of Christianity) is a being of terrible character—cruel, vindictive, capricious and unjust."

"The bill (bill of rights) for establishing religious freedom in the United States, the principles of which had, to a certain degree been enacted before, I had drawn in all of the latitude of reason and right. It still met with opposition; but with some mutilations in the preamble, it was finally passed; and a singular proposition proved that its protection of the opinion was meant to be universal. Where the preamble declares that coercion is a departure from the plan of the holy author of our religion, an amendment was proposed by inserting the words 'Jesus Christ,' so that it should read 'a departure from the plan of Jesus Christ, the holy author of our religion'; the insertion was rejected by a great majority, in proof that they meant to comprehend within the mantle of its protection, the Jew and the Gentile, the Christian and the Mohammedan, the Hindoo and Infidel of every denomination."

And Lincoln, appointed as his commander-in-chief, U. S. Grant, who was almost as outspoken as Jefferson in his antagonism to religion.

The clergy and biographers who are more interested in selling their volumes than arriving at the truth have frequently referred to an alleged speech by Lincoln to a delegation of Baltimore negroes upon their presenting him with a $500.00 bible. They quote Lincoln as saying:*

"In regard to the great book, I have only to say that it is the best gift which God has given to man. All the good from the savior of the world is communicated to us through this book. But for this book we could not know right from wrong. All those things desirable to man are contained in it."

The Washington papers of the time mentioned the visit of this Negro delegation and Lincoln's speech, but did not publish anything like the above quotation. Several months later, this appeared—probably just another Christian forgery. It is interesting to note what Herndon, Lincoln's most intimate friend, says with reference to this. He states:

"I am aware of the fraud committed on Mr. Lincoln in reporting some insane remarks supposed to have been made by him, in 1864, on the presentation of a Bible to him by the colored people of Baltimore. No sane man ever uttered such folly, and no sane man will ever believe it. In that speech Mr. Lincoln is made to say: 'But for this book we could not know right from wrong.' Does any human being believe that Lincoln ever uttered this? What did the whole race of man do to know right from wrong during the countless years that passed before this book was given to the world? How did

* Lincoln Memorial Album, p. 340.

the struggling race of man build up its grand civilizations in the world before this book was given to mankind? What do the millions of people now living, who never heard of this book, do to know how to distinguish right from wrong? Was Lincoln a fool, an ass, a hypocrite, or a combination of them all? or is this speech—this supposed—this fraudulent speech—a lie?"

\*      \*      \*

Two of the chief proofs of Lincoln's religious beliefs used by the clerics are his Gettysburg Address and the Bixby letter—both famous. The first has been characterized by Edgar Lee Masters as a "prose poem" — "Lincoln's most famous utterance" — and the latter, by someone, the "world's most famous letter."

The Gettysburg Address, as usually published, carried the phrase "under God" in the last paragraph; however, this expression was not in the address as delivered at the battlefield memorial exercises. It was later interpolated; whether at the instigation of some of the religious members of Lincoln's cabinet—as in the case of the religious phrase in the Emancipation Proclamation—or in some other manner seems impossible at this date to determine. At any rate it was not in the copy which Lincoln held when he delivered the address.

The Bixby letter has been the occasion of much comment and admirably serves to illustrate the maudlin hysteria so frequently displayed in regard to Lincoln. The letter follows:

"To Mrs. Bixby, Boston, Mass.
"Dear Madam:
"I have been shown in the files of the War Department a statement of the Adjutant General

of Massachusetts that you are the mother of five sons who have died gloriously on the field of battle. I feel how weak and fruitless must be any word of mine which should attempt to beguile you from the grief of a loss so overwhelming. But I cannot refrain from tendering you the consolation that may be found in the thanks of the republic they died to save. I pray that our Heavenly Father may assuage the anguish of your bereavement, and leave you only the cherished memory of the loved and lost, and the solemn pride that must be yours to have laid so costly a sacrifice upon the altar of freedom.

"Yours very sincerely and respectfully,

(signed) A. LINCOLN"

For many years Mrs. Bixby was number one American mother. Finally the investigations of Wakefield and others reveal the following facts in regard to this celebrated case:

a. Widow Bixby of Mass. had five sons in the Union army (this is about the only thing true of the original story);

b. Mrs. Bixby opposed the enlistment of at least some of her sons;

c. Two only, of the sons, were killed in battle;

d. One son was captured, paroled and discharged;

e. Two sons deserted to the enemy and later left the country, one remaining away, deserting wife and children;

f. One of the sons enlisted for a bounty of $325.00;

g. The celebrated letter was not written by Lincoln, but by John Hay, Lincoln's secretary. It is doubtful if Lincoln ever saw it.

h. The first facsimiles of the letter did not appear until 1891 and were patent forgeries, as they were not in the handwriting of Lincoln or Hay.

In view of the above facts, the use of this letter as religious propaganda in regard to Lincoln turns out to be another Christian fiasco. Such hysteria is to be expected of the clergy; however, in the case of Lincoln, it is not confined to religious propaganda. For example, Viscount Bryce said of this letter, "Deep must be the fountains from which there issues so pure a stream." In this case the fountain turns out to be Private Secretary Hay, rather than the "divinely inspired" Lincoln. Carl Sandburg is likewise caught in the same emotional morass. So with thousands of others who have gotten themselves into such an ecstatic state of mind over Lincoln that any approach to any question concerning him stimulates only an emotional complex—reason never entering the picture. Demagogues, both political and religious, constantly use the name of Lincoln to sway the mob. If a saying of Lincoln can be twisted to apply, the case is definitely settled for 90% of the audience.

In connection with the Bixby letter, Wakefield has suggested that in its stead may be used a letter *really written by Lincoln* to Miss Fanny McCullough anent the death of Colonel McCullough who was killed in battle. Compare the following with the Bixby letter:

"Dear Fanny:
"It is with deep grief that I learn of the death of your brave and kind father; and, especially, that it is affecting your young heart beyond what is common in such cases. In this sad world of ours, sorrow comes to all; and, to the young, it comes with bitterest agony, because it takes them unawares. The older have learned to ever expect it.

I am anxious to afford some alleviation of your present distress. Perfect relief is not possible, except with time. You cannot realize that you will ever feel better. Is not this so? And yet it is a mistake. You are sure to be happy again. To know this, which is certainly true, will make you some less miserable now. I have had experience enough to know what I say; and you need only to believe it, to feel better at once. The memory of your dear father, instead of an agony, will yet be a sad, sweet feeling in your heart, of a purer, and holier sort than you have known before.

"Please present my kind regards to your afflicted mother.

"Your sincere friend,

(signed)  A. LINCOLN"

An interesting feature of this thoroughly secular letter is that it was written only a short time following the death of the president's son Willie, at which time the orthodox were claiming Lincoln was "especially turning to religion."

"Yet in spite of the nearness of the latest tragedy in his own life and in spite of the interpretation put upon it by many, there is no appeal to God, no reference to immortality, and no religious background in the letter. It is a simple but lofty effort of one human being to assuage the apparently hopeless grief of another human being by showing that her sorrow will not be endless and that she will again be happy. It could not fail to be of great help to the bereaved, and I consider it to be far superior to the Bixby letter." (Wakefield.)

Lyman Abbott refers to Lincoln as an agnostic, but a "religious agnostic," whom Abbott thinks put his faith in a supreme being "because God is good." Abbott, also, thinks him religious because "a life of service and self sacrifice leads through doubt to faith," yet Abbott admits Lincoln wrote an essay or dissertation against Christianity which Abbott says was "fortunately" thrown into the fire. Lincoln, doubtless, would have been greatly interested in Abbott's logic—or lack of it.

As an example of clerical balderdash over Lincoln, attention may be called to a memorial sermon delivered April 15, 1865, by Rev. W. T. Wilson, in St. Peter's Church, which sermon was printed in pamphlet form and widely circulated.

Rev. Wilson, in his opening paragraph, says, "how sudden and appalling the disaster that has fallen upon the nation!" Further, in his discourse he states that, "the death of Abraham Lincoln was an untimely death, an inscrutable dispensation of Providence, a great national disaster." It may be somewhat puzzling to understand how Lincoln's untimely death, which is a great national disaster, can at the same time be a dispensation of Providence, for this same cleric has assured us that Providence is intent upon preserving this nation. However, in closing his sermon, the Reverend makes this clear (to one with a religious mentality) by pointing out that, "We cannot doubt that in the permission of that deed (the assassination of Lincoln) God had a wise and far reaching purpose . . . Perhaps it was to secure us from the immoderation of victory, and lead us to wait humbly upon that Providence from whom all victory comes."*

---

* Rev. G. W. Prince of Detroit states Lincoln's assassination "compels us to admit that there is a Providence that governs," while Rev. H. P. Tappan of Berlin asks, "Who can say that this new lesson (Lincoln's assassination) was not needed to prevent the generosity and kindness which sprang up in the path of victory from degenerating into a weakness that might leave the country open to new perils?", a rather characteristic Christian attitude, we'll have to admit.

Can it be expected that people will take a rational view of an historical event under the stimulus of such —— —— ——?

Is not the analytical and scholarly statement of Masters more refreshing:

"More profoundly searched, his negative psychology, his analytical defensiveness, his constant attitude which demanded proof from the affirmative side, his coldness, his realism, his intellectual detachment, his separateness from the mob, which made him indifferent to local interests and politics, and no doubt a certain intellectual pride which came to him in the New Salem days and gave him belief that he was different from other men, as he was,—all these things operated to keep Lincoln out of the church. Nor did he weakly yield to public opinion and join a church, even when it would have been of advantage to him in politics to have done so."

Masters also makes the following illuminating statements:

"The idea that Lincoln struggled on through poverty and adversity, holding to ideals, and without luck anywhere along the way, and that it was only a great moral impulse of God's truth, marching on, which chose him to do God's work is one of the entrancing myths with which people love to bewitch themselves after first having created it."

"Strange is it that it was Lincoln who was the first president to introduce the cant and the hypocrisy of Christianity into American politics."

(In this Masters may be a bit unfair, for many of the religious expressions with which Lincoln is credited were interpolated by religious zealots in his official family, to whom he doubtless yielded rather than stir up a controversy and divert people's attention from the main issue.)

Beneath Lincoln's calm, cold exterior there existed a certain emotional strain which at times overpowered his judgment. This tendency to, occasionally "slop over" and do illogical things happened not infrequently, especially after he became an administrative. The progress of the war, the administration of justice, the making of appointments all suffered more or less from this weakness in Lincoln's nature. At the same time, it rendered him more human (i.e. more like the average uncontrolled and uneducated mind of the mediocre) and endeared him to the common man. In his position as president, there were many events, many situations, which would arouse the emotions of such an one as Lincoln. Under the stress of these, he occasionally would use certain conventional theological expressions, such as "trust in providence," "thank God," "may our prayers be answered," etc., probably with about as much intellectual significance as one's expression, "Great Caesar," "Good Heavens," et cetera.* Certainly the heedless use of these religious expressions can scarcely be considered as evidence of a devout religious belief in the face of such a statement as that deliberately made upon the subject in Lincoln's letter to his intimate friend, Judge Wakefield.

---

* Santyana in discussing the absence of religion in Shakespeare affords an explanation: "There are, indeed, numerous exclamations and invocations in Shakespeare which we, who have other means of information, know to be evidences of current religious ideas. Shakespeare adopts these, as he adopts the rest of his vocabulary, from the society about him. But he seldom or never gives them their original value. . . . Oaths are the fossils of piety. The geologist recognizes in them the relics of a once active devotion, but they are now only counters and pebbles tossed about in the unconscious play of expression. The lighter and more constant their use, the less their meaning."

Lincoln is—each year, since his death—becoming more and more religious. For example, if we compare his biography in the Encyclopedia Brittanica of today with that of a generation ago, a marked change is noted. In the earlier editions, religion is not even mentioned, while now a specious argument is entered upon to prove him religious. So in other writings. (See foot note p. 58.)

If Lincoln was chosen by God as His inspired agent, can we in any manner benefit from a study of his acts? Just what inspiration can one get from the doings of a demigod? Even assuming that such a thing as a demigod might exist, you and I can never become demigods. Therefore, the deeds and performances of a demigod have no lesson for us ordinary mortals, regardless of our ability or our efforts. We cannot aspire to the record of a demigod, for we are only human. We can, therefore, obtain only discouragement from the acts and accomplishments of such an one.

By the same token, we are afforded no inspiration or encouragement from the record of Lincoln if he constantly received supernatural aid. In such a case, his deeds become not his own but those of the god to whom he appeals in his "frequent prayers." It, to be sure, may be argued that we may at any time call upon the Almighty, again assuming that there may exist such a being, and He may answer our supplications. Would you wish to turn the management of your important business over to one who in advance informed you that he expected to accomplish his results by depending upon divine guidance? Obviously we expect the man— the human being—to do the work—do the work as a competent and conscientious human being—overcome his obstacles by his own skill and effort. If, then, he accomplishes great results, we are afforded an example to emulate. We may be inspired to attempt the attainment of like results, and if we have the requisite ability and training, we may look forward to like accomplishments.

Therefore, I say, our inspiration from Lincoln must be from the fact that he was an ordinary or perhaps an *extraordinary* man, but not one who was divinely inspired, or one who has the ability to secure supernatural aid. We are also confronted with an anomaly equally absurd in these same Pharisees being horrified at the idea of Lincoln (or his mother) being natural children, yet they will accept without any qualms the long line of honored English sovereigns descended from the bastard William the Conqueror. One also wonders if they know their leading ecclesiastical work of art—the Lord's Supper—was painted by a natural child, who is far greater than his celebrated painting in a multitude of other fields of human activity; in fact is one of the rare geniuses of all time. Do we honor him any the less because he did not consult us in the selection of a father?

Do we enjoy the magnificent literary productions of Dumas any less because he was a bastard, or enjoy the exquisite music of Borodin less because his parents had not complied with our ideas of proper form and ceremony? Was D'Alembert any less a scientist born out of wedlock? Do the many admirers of Napoleon think more or less of him because of his doubtful paternity? Was Alexander Hamilton any less a financier and patriot as a result of being a bastard? Or the celebrated work of Erasmus any less valuable for the same reason?

Yet Washington appointed Hamilton as his secretary of the treasury. How very astounding that the "pious, praying" Washington should appoint an infidel as secretary of state and a bastard as

secretary of the treasury in his first cabinet. In
view of this, why look askance at Lincoln's ques-
tionable ancestry?

\* \* \*

One of the most disgraceful features of the Lincoln hysteria has been its abuse of Herndon. This
amazing attitude of the clergy is apparently
motivated solely from Herndon's desire to publish
the truth about Lincoln, for Herndon was a gentleman and a scholar—patriotic, democratic, tolerant
and honest to a fault.  Even if he made a few mistakes in his Lincoln chronology (and it has not been
shown he did) his motives could never be ques-
tioned. Probably no man lived whom Lincoln held
in higher esteem. The slanderous attacks upon him
by the clergy, therefore, form another ugly blot
upon the pages of Lincoln history—a blot which
the honest and tolerant Lincoln would have been
first to resent, a blot which—had it occurred during his lifetime—would have caused Lincoln more
distress and pain than any of the numerous ridiculous episodes told of him. Herndon was morally and
intellectually so far above those who now attempt
to make capital by vilifying him that they scarcely
appear human by comparison.

Since the recent publication of Hertz' "Hidden
Lincoln" and Newton's "Lincoln and Herndon," we
know considerably more of Lincoln. These two, together with the biographies of Lamon, Beverage,
and Herndon and Week, furnish the facts of Lincoln's life with which a rational biography can be
written.

\* \* \*

One of the remarkable characteristics of the
human kind — even the supposed intellectual
stratum of the same — is its habit of speaking in
a thoughtless and irrational manner.  In 1882,

O. H. Oldroyd, an admirer of Lincoln and a collector of Lincoln relics, conceived the idea of compiling an album of opinions of Lincoln. He solicited the brief opinions of 200 people, who were more or less prominent, and published their opinions in the "Lincoln Memorial Album of Immortelles." It would seem that such a compilation might have been of real value. Alas; the work is almost as barren of ideas as a blank page. Each contributor evidently thought he must apotheosize, with the result that the album is a mass of maudlin, mawkish parroting, and its value is practically nil, except as a study of mob psychology. There is scarcely a critical statement in the volume of over 500 pages—not an attempt at scientific, historical approach. Unfortunately, much of our Lincoln literature tends to be of this type.

Reference has been made to Holland's fabulous life of Lincoln. Seven years after Lincoln's death, Ward H. Lamon published his "Life of Abraham Lincoln." Holland reviewed Lamon's biography at great length in Scribners for August of that year. This review was so intemperate, so filled with jealousy and calumny for Lamon and his associates that it will condemn Holland for all time. A comparison of the two biographers can best be made by quoting a review from the New York World at the time, which states:

"Mr. Ward H. Lamon is the author of one 'Life of Lincoln,' and Dr. J. G. Holland is the author of another. Mr. Lamon was the intimate personal and political friend of Mr. Lincoln, trusting and trusted, from the time of their joint practice in the Illinois Quarter Sessions to the moment of Mr. Lincoln's death at Washington. Dr. Holland was nothing to Mr. Lincoln—neither known nor knowing. Dr. Holland rushed his 'Life' from the press

before the disfigured corpse was fairly out of
sight, while the public mind lingered with horror
over the details of the tragedy, and, excited by
morbid curiosity, was willing to pay for its grati-
fication. Mr. Lamon waited many years, until all
adventitious interest had subsided, and then with
incredible labor and pains, produced a volume
founded upon materials which, for their fulness,
variety, and seeming authenticity are unrivaled in
the history of biographies. Dr. Holland's single volume professed to cover the whole of Mr. Lincoln's
career. Mr. Lamon's single volume was modestly
confined tó part of it. Dr. Holland's was an easy,
graceful, off- hand performance, having but the
one slight demerit of being in all essential partic-
ulars untrue from beginning to end. Mr. Lamon's
was a labored, cautious, and carefully verified narrative which seems to have been accepted by dis-
interested critics as entirely authentic.

"Dr. Holland would probably be very much
shocked if anybody should ask him to bear false
witness in favor of his neighbor in a court of justice, but he takes up his pen to make a record which
he hopes and intends shall endure forever, and in
that record deliberately bears false witness in
favor of a public man whom he happened to admire,
with no kind of offense to his serene and 'cultured'
conscience. If this were all—if Dr. Holland merely
asserted his own right to compose and publish
elaborate fictions on historical subjects—we might
comfort ourselves with the reflection that such
literature is likely to be as evanescent as it is dis-
honest, and let him pass in silence. But this is not
all. He maintains that it is everybody's duty to
help him to deceive the public and to write down
his more conscientious competitor. He turns up the
nose of 'culture' and curls the lip of 'art' at Mr.

Lamon's homely narrative of facts, and gravely insists that all other noses and all other lips shall be turned up and curled because his are. He implores the public, which he insulted and gulled with his own book, to damn Mr. Lamon's, and he puts his request on the very ground that Mr. Lamon has stupidly gone and narrated undeniable truths, whereby he has demolished an empty shrine that was profitable to many, and broken a painted idol that might have served for a god.

"The names of Holland and Lamon are not of themselves and by themselves illustrious; but starting from the title-pages of the two Lives of Lincoln, and representing, as they do, the two schools of biography writers, the one stands for a principle and the other for the want of it."

Edgar Lee Masters has furnished us with one of the few rational analyses we have had of Lincoln since the publications of Lamon and Herndon. His "Lincoln the Man" is anything but an apotheosis. In fact it, at times, appears a bit unfair to Lincoln, and some of Masters' deductions may seem somewhat far fetched. The book will frequently impart a real shock to the Lincoln idolaters—if they read it. To the student of history and biography, however, it forms a most refreshing oasis in the desert of Lincolniana, so dearth of thought, and will be a valuable asset even though the waters of its springs may be a bit acrid and irritating to the supersensitive hero worshipers. Masters, in referring to Lincoln's habit of shifting position politically, says, "Vainly shall we expect Lincoln to be consistent intellectually at any time; he remained the same divided mind to the last day of his life, who in the same speech, and sometimes in the same letter presented the antinomy of his nature."

Lincoln's indecision was often his undoing.

This indecision was at times apparently due to lack of courage and at other times due to an apparent lack of judgment—or perhaps both. For example, in his appointment of Cameron to the position of Secretary of War; the appointment was made and withdrawn, again made and confirmed, to be followed by Cameron's dismissal and his appointment as ambassador to Russia. Yet Lincoln had been warned in advance of the character of Cameron. Again and again his wavering, vacillating habits caused him no end of trouble and probably materially prolonged the war.

\*    \*    \*

It may be interesting in passing to note another popular illusion in regard to Lincoln. The average American thinks he spent most of his youthful days splitting rails. There is little evidence that he did anything of consequence in this line. Early in 1860, Lincoln was mentioned as a possible candidate for the Vice Presidency on a ticket with William H. Seward. However, young Richard Oglesby, and some of his friends, had a different notion. Their work and the origin of the rail splitting story is best told by Mrs. Jane Martin Johns in her "Personal Recollections, 1849-1865":—

"To Oglesby, of Decatur, must be conceded the honor of *creating* the candidacy of Abraham Lincoln for president of the United States. He knew and honored and loved Mr. Lincoln, and believed from the bottom of his great heart that none of the other candidates were so eminently fitted for that high position as Abraham Lincoln. He had conceived the idea of presenting Lincoln as the representative candidate of free labor, the exponent of the possibilities for a poor man in a free state. Recalling the successful Log Cabin and Hard Cider campaign of 1840, he determined to find some one thing in Mr. Lincoln's unsuccessful career as a worker that could be made the emblem of that idea, and a catch word which would make enthusiastic the working people. One day he met John Hanks, whom he knew had worked with Lincoln on a farm years and years before, and asked him 'what kind of work "Abe" used to be good at.'

" 'Well, not much of any kind but dreaming,' was Hanks' reply, 'but he did help me split a lot of rails when we made the clearing twelve miles west of here.'

"The rest of the story I will give as it was related to J. McCan Davis, clerk of the Supreme Court of Illinois, by Mr. Oglesby himself:

" 'John,' said I, 'did you split rails down there with Old Abe?'

" 'Yes; every day,' he replied.

" 'Do you suppose you could find any of them now?'

" 'Yes,' he said, 'The last time I was down there, ten years ago, there were plenty of them left.'

" 'What are you going to do tomorrow?'

" 'Nothing.'

" 'Then,' said I, 'come around and get in my buggy and we will drive down there.'

"So the next day we drove out to the old clearing. We turned in by the timber, and John said:

" 'Dick, if I don't find any black-walnut rails, nor any honey-locust rails, I won't claim it's the fence Abe and I built.'

"Presently John said: 'There's the fence!'

" 'But look at those great trees,' said I.

" 'Certainly,' he answered. 'They have all grown up since.'

"John got out, I stayed in the buggy. John kneeled down and commenced chipping the rails of the old fence with a penknife. Soon he came back with black-walnut shavings and honey-locust shavings.

" 'There they are;' he said, triumphantly holding out the shavings. 'They are the identical rails we made.'

"Then I got out and made an examination of the fence. There were many black-walnut and honey-locust rails.

" 'John,' said I, "where did you get these rails?'

" 'I can take you to the stumps,' he answered.

" 'We will go down there,' said I.

"We drove about a hundred yards.

" 'Now, said he, 'look! There's a black-walnut stump; there's another—another—another. Here's where we cut the trees down and split the rails. Then we got a horse and wagon, hauled them in, and built the fence and the cabin.'

"We took two of the rails and tied them under the hind axle-tree of my new buggy, and started for town. People would occasionally pass and think something had broken. We let them think so, for we didn't wish to tell anybody just what we were doing. We kept right on until we got to my barn. There we hid the rails until the day of the convention.

"Before the convention met, I talked with several Republicans about my plans, and we fixed it up that old John Hanks should take the rails into the convention. We made a banner, attached to a board across the top of the rails, with the inscription:

" 'Abraham Lincoln, The Railsplitter Candidate, for President in 1860. Two rails from a lot of 3,000 made in 1830 by John Hanks and Abe Lincoln.'

"After the convention got under way, I arose and announced that the old Democrat desired to make a contribution to the convention. The proceedings stopped, and all was expectancy and excitement. Then in walked old John with the banner on the rails.

"From that time forward the rails were ever present in the campaign."

"The Seward boom was dead. 'Dick' Oglesby and old John Hanks and two fence rails had killed it.

"John M. Palmer was soon on his feet with a resolution declaring that 'Abraham Lincoln is the first choice of the Republican party of Illinois for the presidency,' and instructing 'the delegates to the Chicago convention to use all honorable means to secure the nomination and to cast the vote of the state as a unit for him.'"

Mrs. Johns, who was personally acquainted with Lincoln, relates a number of interesting events of his career, but says nothing of any religious activity and nothing to indicate his selection as a candidate involved anything of the supernatural.

Likewise Sherman Day Wakefield, in his recent book, "How Lincoln Became President," details how it was done by the ordinary political methods and tricks of controlling a convention, together with play upon mob psychology. If Jehovah was in control of this convention, Wakefield did not discover it—and it might also be added that Wakefield's grandfather was an intimate of Lincoln and attended the convention.

\*    \*    \*

Lincoln was most clever at winning men's good will. He had a happy faculty of getting all classes and conditions of men to aid him in his undertak-

ings.  The pious and the preachers were no ex-
ception to this.  During the war he needed the help
of all, and showed his good judgment in not alienat-
ing the friendship of a group as intolerant, and
vociferous as the clergy.*

Furthermore, it should be borne in mind that
Lincoln was probably at all times painfully con-
scious of his deficiencies—his lack of education, experience and cultural background.  He must frequently have felt himself seriously unfitted for the
high position he held, and his subconscious mind
must have frequently led him to resort to religious
artifice or humorous story to meet a situation with
which he was mentally unable to cope at the time.

Innumerable fables are constantly being published concerning Lincoln. One of the over-worked
ones is concerning his mother's funeral. The story
of Lincoln—at age 9—writing to a minister to
come and preach a funeral sermon on his mother,
then leaving her grave unmarked and uncared for
throughout his life of 56 years, is curious.  The
framing of the former fable and the omission to
mention the latter neglect on the part of the
popular biographers, forms an interesting picture
of the mental and moral make up of these
biographers.

Recently a new story has appeared to the effect
that Lincoln's parents, while in Kentucky, were
reasonably prosperous, or at least in comfortable
circumstances.  It will be interesting to compare

---

* Lincoln's attitude toward our silly Thanksgiving Day
is characteristic. From the time Thomas Jefferson refused
to make himself ridiculous by the issuance of a Thanksgiving Day proclamation to the time of Lincoln, no such
proclamation was issued.  Lincoln, however, yielded to
pressure and issued one with the comment that it "pleases
the fools."

this with Lincoln's own statement to his friend Swett:

"I can remember our life in Kentucky; the cabin, the stinted living (sic), the sale of our possessions, and the journey with my father and mother to Southern Indiana." (Lincoln to Leonard Swett in Rice's "Reminiscences of Abraham Lincoln.") In this connection it is interesting to note that he makes no mention of his sister.

\*    \*    \*

In making an appraisal of Lincoln or Lincoln's influence, it is difficult to know who is the more unfortunate victim, Lincoln or the innocent public.

Lincoln was an honest and upright citizen of noble and generous character, who is entitled to a certain amount of respect from Americans — especially lovers of human freedom. Even if he is not one of the world's greatest, he may be accorded the credit due a good citizen in a high and responsible position making an honest effort with a moderate degree of success. It is, however, scarcely in order to apotheosize, canonize or in any other manner make him appear ridiculous. The fact that he rose from a lowly station in life to the exalted position as head of a great nation, that he played an important part in winning a great war, that he was given credit for freeing many millions of human beings from slavery, yet through it all put on no imperial airs, but remained at all times the plain, honest, unassuming, democratic citizen as before, will ever endear him to Americans.

The unfortunate and defenseless public, however, is almost powerless to protect itself from Lincoln hysteria. If it attempts to get the truth about Lincoln, it is confronted with a mountain of fable and froth, foolishness and fancy, through which it must dig to obtain, only an occasional gem of truth—and even after a truth has been obtained, doubt may now be thrown around this truth by an over-powering blast of vulgar advertising propaganda. As the public welters in a morass of balderdash and buncombe, it is little wonder that discouragement and distrust may finally overcome the honest efforts to unscramble fact from fable.

If an honest citizen wishes to teach his son something of the great men of the American nation, he may approach the public library only to find many of the great men represented with few, if any, biographies, whereas he will find several shelves of Lincoln books — most of the latter not worth the paper upon which they are printed. He may wisely divert the impressionable mind from this collection of maudlin propaganda, but it is almost impossible to protect the innocent youth from the tommyrot of the birthday celebration.

It is one of the tragedies of the present age that the truth concerning great men is so difficult to obtain, for biographies are chiefly a mass of prejudices and preconceived notions, flavored with cheap, extravagant eulogy and petty praise. (Probably the present age *only* should not be charged with this.) We might learn a lesson or two from the lives of great men if biographers would only tell the truth rather than make their books a mass of propaganda.

Of the thousands of books published on Lincoln, one can almost count on his fingers those of any value as critical, scientific productions. How, in view of this, is the uninformed reader to arrive at the truth? The problem is a difficult one. The reader's own gullibility makes him the profitable victim of the unscrupulous publisher and the crusading propagandist who prepares the publication. The schools of the country might do much to correct this condition, but our educators are too afraid of meddlesome preachers and professional patriots to risk their positions in behalf of the truth.

It is said that "truth makes the devil blush," but a birthday "orator" may be ever so careless with it without the slightest blush.

\*    \*    \*

By a strange turn of fortune's wheel, Lincoln's ambition coincided with the inevitable trend of events leading to the abolition of human slavery. That he made some contribution to this important event is evident, but the part he played in this was more fortuitous than intentional, for this fact must not be overlooked—Lincoln, at the time of his nomination for president, was *not* in favor of the abolition of slavery. Neither was he in favor of going to war, yet he unwittingly did more probably than any other individual to bring on the immediate conflict, on account of his social standing— or lack of it.  Had, for example, Douglas been elected president in 1860, a compromise of some nature with the South might have been possible and the bloody war averted.  However, with Lincoln as president, the Southern aristocrat (and it must be remembered that the southern aristocrats were the government) had no method of approach. As well ask him to sit down at a conference table with a negro as with a "poh white." A conference or a compromise was thus *impossible.*

No one, of course, can know what turn American national events would have taken had there been no civil war, but it is interesting to speculate upon the results.  That there would have been saved several million valuable lives and several billions of money goes without saying. But the secondary effects were even more disastrous and far reaching—the enmity and sectional hatred which arose, the political oligarchy of ex soldiers with their disgusting pension raids upon the public treasury (a custom carried over to later wars) and a monopoly by them of political offices, a false and distorted idea of patriotism, the retardation to the material development of the South, the racial hatred between southern blacks and whites greatly exaggerated, and many other baneful effects. In other words, the secondary effects of this, as of all wars, were more vicious and far reaching in cost of moral, physical and economic debasement than the first cost in blood and money.

To these secondary effects is now added the debasing moral effect of presenting to the innocent youth of the land the account of a prominent national character of this period in an utterly false light.

*     *     *

Bacon has said that no mind, however capable, is able to examine a matter which is contrary to its early teachings until it is freed of its prejudices and preconceived notions. It is hoped this brief statement may aid in sweeping away some of the erroneous predilections and prejudices, some of the emotional trash and tripe with reference to Lincoln.

# INDEX

Abbott, Lyman, 65, 66.
Abolitionist, 23.
Adams, 59.
Administrative, Lincoln as, 14, 68.
Adventist Herald, 43.
Advertising, 20, 81.
Album of Immortelles, "Lincoln Memorial", 72.
Allen, Ethan, 42.
American politics, 67.
Ammonites, 37.
Ancestry of Lincoln, 20, 26.
Anti-slavery, 14, 54, 56.
Apologists for Lincoln, 45.
Apotheosis of Lincoln, 12.
Aristocracy, Southern, 23.
Aristocrats, Southern, 22, 82.
Assassination of Lincoln, 66.

Bacon, 83.
Ballot, for negro, 21.
Baltimore, 25.
Baltimore, negroes, 61.
Baptists, 29.
Bar, opinion of Lincoln, 20.
Barbadoes, 23.
Bastards, 26, 70.
Bateman, Newton, 32, 33.
Bates, Ed., 14, 15, 45.
"Behind the Scenes," 44.

Birthday orators, 52.
Bixby, 63.
Bixby letter, 62.
Booth, Edwin, 46.
Booth, J. W., 45.
Borodin, 70.
Boston, 56, 57.
Britt, Albert, 9.
Bryce, Viscount, 64.
Butler, 14, 15.

Cabinet member, unofficial, 19.
Calvin, 60.
Cameron, 75.
Campbellites, 29.
Candidacy of Lincoln for President, 75.
Carpenter, 38.
Carroll, Anna, 18.
Cartwright, Peter, 27, 30, 43, 48.
Chaplain, Neill, 38.
Chase, Secy., 51.
Chastity of Lincoln's Mother, 29.
Chicago convention, 78.
Christ, 19, 31.
Christ-like face of Lincoln, 38.
Christian, 58, 60.